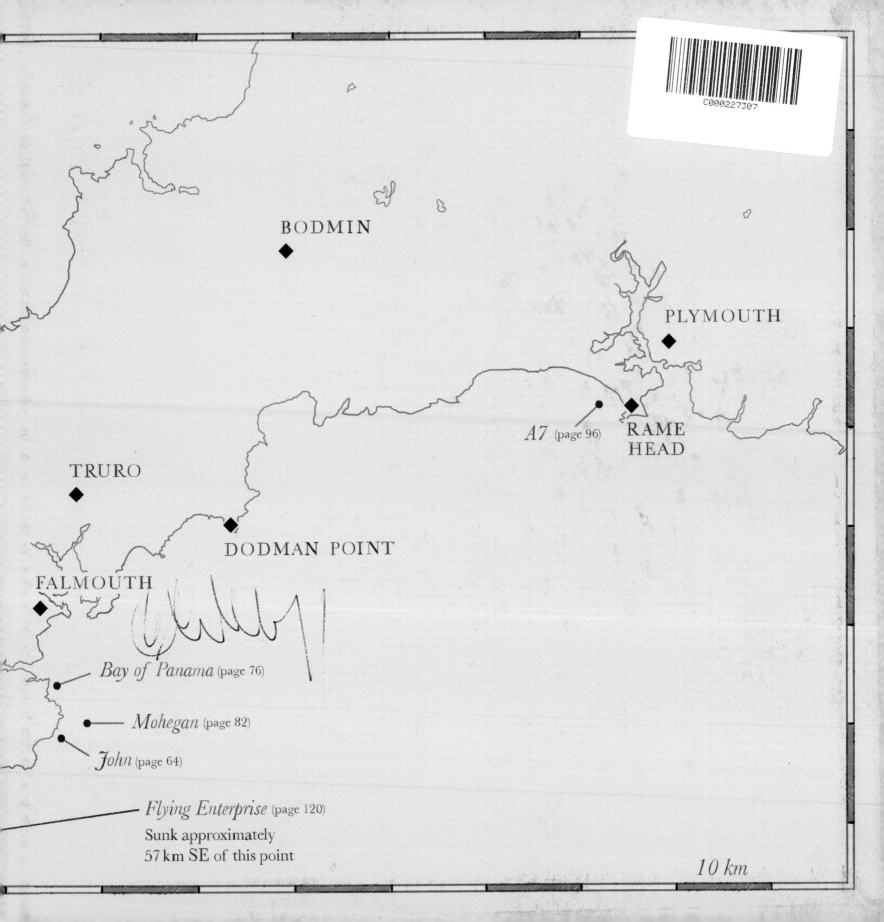

BODMIN

PLYMOUTH

TRURO

A7 (page 96)   RAME
HEAD

DODMAN POINT

FALMOUTH

Bay of Panama (page 76)

Mohegan (page 82)

John (page 64)

Flying Enterprise (page 120)
Sunk approximately
57 km SE of this point

10 km

First published 2019 by Mabecron Books Ltd,

Bristol Orchard, St Mellion, Saltash, Cornwall, PL12 6RQ.

Written by Richard Larn OBE. Illustrated by Oliver Hurst. Designed by Keryn Bibby.

Typeset in Optimus Princeps, Baskerville and Helvetica Neu. Printed in Malaysia.

SEA*of*STORMS

Shipwrecks of Cornwall and the Isles of Scilly

SEA*of*STORMS

Shipwrecks of Cornwall and the Isles of Scilly

RICHARD LARN OBE

ILLUSTRATED BY OLIVER HURST

Illustration credits (© Oliver Hurst):

Cover: Barque *John* (page 64)

Back cover: HM Submarine *A7* (page 96)

Frontispiece: HMS *Warspite* (page 114)

FOREWORD

SIR TIM SMIT

I was raised on stories of marine adventure: Hans and Lotte Haas; Jacques Cousteau; Jacques Piccard and William Beebe. I read about the extraordinary exploits of those who quested to the far-flung reaches of the globe in search of riches, conquest and knowledge. My mind was captured by *Treasure Island*; *Robinson Crusoe*; *Moby Dick*; and tales of Atlantis and cities lost beneath the sea. Above all, Jules Verne was the conductor of my imaginings.

These interests never had a focus until June 1975…

The Ghost Ship loomed up in front of me through the plankton haze, perfectly pinioned between two enormous rocks. The image would linger. The loneliness of this grave offset by the teeming shoals of fish that had made it home; the windowless bridge; the brass binnacle – its glass fractured – both attracted and repelled me. This was the Farne Islands hospital ship, a WW1 torpedo victim…and my introduction to the awe of discovery, a fascination that holds me still.

What is it about a shipwreck? The perils of war, slavery, cannibals and sharks play on the imagination and we can all shiver at being adrift and helpless in a raging storm, the pounding of waves on rocks portending doom. But that is not all. For me, as an archaeologist by training, the magic lies in the fact that almost all shipwrecks are like unedited crime scenes; each a captured moment of time, telling of lives cut short, of dreams, hopes and fears ended at a blow; some almost perfectly preserved, the remains of others so scattered as to be incapable of any form of reassembly in substance or narrative. The greatest shipwrecks have the best narratives and while *Titanic, Lusitania, Royal Oak* and *Bismarck* are household names, it is the quiet tales of tragedy that set in motion great shifts in history, from the wreck of the *Association* to revulsion at the fate of slaves.

Richard and Bridget Larn are heroes of mine. Their brave and pioneering expeditions, with Bridget fearlessly manoeuvring boats through the fearsome Western Rocks in the Isles of Scilly while Richard led the divers below, have contributed to the growing respectability of Maritime Archaeology. They were not alone. We owe a great debt to this group of wreck divers who came together in the late 1960s as fascinated marine detectives, transforming the occupation into a reputable science over the next 30 years. It is through their work that so many of the stories that have a grip on our imagination have artefacts to give our dreams substance.

This marvellous book, with its rich and well-judged illustrations by Oliver Hurst, captures perfectly the agony of loss; the ever-present background music of jeopardy that accompanies marine adventures; the acts of bravery and stupidity; and a whole world of 'what ifs?' and 'if onlys'. Some of these extraordinary tragedies leave their melancholy testimony in the many graves in our coastal churchyards, dedicated to the memory of those in peril on the sea. That, they surely were. But their stories live on.

INTRODUCTION

This is a book about ships that came to grief on the three different coastlines of Cornwall, its infamous north and south coasts and the remote Isles of Scilly, over a period of almost 500 years. Cornwall and the Isles of Scilly have a dramatic history of shipwrecks, and lurid – and mostly apocryphal – stories have always circulated of clifftop lanterns tied to donkey's tails and cargo-strewn beaches being pillaged by wreckers. How many ships have foundered on Cornwall's rugged coastline is still an educated guess, since records prior to 1500 AD are scarce, but we know of at least 5,700. Of these some 2,400 were lost on the south coast, 2,300 on the north and 1,000 on the Isles of Scilly.

Sea of Storms is divided into three sections: 'The Age of Sail', recounting the tales of seven shipwrecks which took place between 1527 and 1798; 'Sail Gives Way to Steam', reflecting a century of great change between 1807 and 1907; and 'The Era of Modern Technology', which selects eight examples from just before World War 1 right up to the beginning of the 21st century. Twenty-one stories have been chosen and are re-told by Richard Larn, OBE, who has devoted a lifetime to exploring the many and varied aspects of Cornwall's maritime heritage and shipwreck history. Each story is illustrated with oil paintings and drawings by Oliver Hurst, who graduated with a degree in Illustration from University College Falmouth (now Falmouth University) in 2006 and has since forged a successful career as a book and magazine illustrator, specialising in marine subjects.

Most of the historic shipwrecks featured in this book are comparatively recent re-discoveries, their locations explored as a result of the post-World War 2 expansion of interest in British maritime archaeology and facilitated by advances in diving equipment. Previously it was thought that (unlike in the non-tidal Mediterranean) historic shipwrecks could not survive in British waters 'where storms, fierce currents and teredo worm would collectively destroy wooden ship remains within a few years'. All this changed during the 1940s when the most famous underwater explorer of recent times, Jacques-Yves Cousteau (1910–1997), together with the French engineer Émile Gagnan, pioneered the innovation of modern underwater diving through their work on adapting and improving a 19th-century breathing apparatus called the 'Regulateur', enabling extended periods of time to be spent underwater.

Left: Full-rigged ship *Bay of Panama* (page 76)

After the war, Cousteau's and Gagnan's patented invention was sold to Britain and the USA under the name 'Aqualung', and overnight anyone could take up diving and underwater exploration. The British Sub-Aqua Club was formed in 1953 and its members began to locate vast numbers of sunken ships, both old and new, around the British coastline. Maritime archaeology and amateur salvage in Britain soon became a reality and some spectacular wrecks, such as Henry VIII's warship the *Mary Rose*, which sank in the Solent in 1545, were re-discovered.

The author's personal choice of the shipwrecks included in this book reflects his own experience as a diver over an astonishing 67-year span. Richard Larn taught himself to dive in the River Thames in 1947, having bought two sets of government-surplus submarine escape apparatus, developed for German U-boats by Dräger of Lübeck, for 10 shillings (50p) each. He went on to become a Chief Petty Officer diver in the Royal Navy and in 1956 was appointed to Malta where he built his own 'Aqualung' after modifying a Calor Gas regulator, gas mask hoses and aircraft oxygen cylinders. His early experience of diving shipwrecks was along the Maltese coast, where he looked at previously known sites and found many new ones. After returning to the UK in 1960, he went on to help discover or work on all seven of the historic wrecks in Part 1 'The Age of Sail', of which the Portuguese galleon *St Anthony*, which sank off the Lizard in 1527 (see pages 14 to 19), is the earliest identifiable shipwreck on which he has dived.

Later Richard set up Prodive Ltd, a commercial diving company based in Charlestown, Cornwall, and at Falmouth Docks, where he helped train hundreds of government-selected candidates in achieving professional diving qualifications. In 1976, he and his wife Bridget, in partnership with Roy and Joan Davis, opened the Charlestown Shipwreck Centre, which became the largest collection of shipwreck artefacts in the UK (now in the safe hands of Sir Tim Smit, founder of the Eden Project), creating a maritime legacy for future generations to enjoy.

Both the author and the illustrator have worked closely together to bring to life each story in words and pictures, drawing on contemporary archives, eye-witness accounts and historic paintings to illuminate the period and to give a taste of the tragedy and heroism, misadventure, carelessness, greed or ignorance, which lie behind each shipwreck. In his own words, Oliver Hurst describes the historical, technical and human challenges he encountered in producing visual interpretations of such varied and dramatic experiences:

'Being asked to reconstruct these incredible stories is something that any artist would consider quite an undertaking, and an honour. From the harrowing scenes on board the barque 'John' ('189 Emigrant Passengers Drowned', pages 64 to 69) to the gallantry of Captain Carlsen of the 'Flying Enterprise' ('The Captain who Stayed with his Ship', pages 120 to 125), the process of recreating each of these tales in pictures has been, for me, an immersive and educational story of its own.

'An oil painting requires a lot of preparation and forethought. Research, referencing, historical accuracy, composition, tone and palette are all matters that I like to get resolved in advance. I wanted the paintings themselves to fit together as a body of work, but also to reflect the era in which the stories they represent occurred. This meant adjusting the colour palette to the rich, dark nocturnes of the 17th-century Dutch masters in my painting of the Dutch fluyt 'Schiedam' ('Captured by Pirates', pages 26 to 31), and to the almost mono-chromatic neutrals of the early Impressionists for the 'Bay of Panama' ('Frozen to Death in the Rigging', pages 76 to 81). I maintained most of the same core colours for every painting to give the whole book its binding atmosphere, but made small adjustments to fit my principle of era-specific representation.

As well as deciding on colour and composition, it is necessary to think about the audience. With this in mind, I was very wary about how to depict some of the more human scenes. While striving to attain historical accuracy, and maintaining a human connection to these ships, I thought it best to be sensitive to the memories of all those who lost their lives. One instance is that of Admiral Sir Clowdisley Shovell in the 'Association' wreck ('The Loss of Sir Clowdisley Shovell's Flagship', pages 32 to 37). It is unlikely that he would have been wearing his wig and even if he had, it almost certainly would not have stayed on his head during his last storm-tossed hours, but I thought it was appropriate to shroud his face with it. The wig gives the depiction of his body some dignity and suggests his rank and status. A similar problem arose with the representation of the loss of RNLB 'Solomon Browne' and MV 'Union Star' (The Penlee Disaster', pages 132 to 141), in a way which would not sensationalise the tragedy which is still so raw in the memories of many people. After much discussion, we agreed that the illustration needed to combine accuracy with sensitivity, while paying tribute to the staggering bravery of the seamen and airmen who strove so hard to try to avert the catastrophe on that fateful night.

'There are a few moments of artistic licence throughout this book, but the core aim was always to represent these remarkable stories as accurately as possible, whether it is the markings on a WW1 submarine or the exact rock formations of a particular Cornish cove.'

Happily, in modern times, the disaster of shipwrecks has become a much rarer event. As each story unfolds, it is shown that developments in ship design over the centuries have helped ships to resist the vagaries of our ever-changing weather and the destructive power of the sea. The loss of Sir Clowdisley Shovell's fleet in 1707 resulted some years later in the discovery of Longitude, enabling navigators to plot their course more accurately, and the wreck of HMS *Anson* within sight of shore in Mount's Bay in 1807 ('The Wreck that Saved 10,000 Lives', pages 58 to 63) led directly to the invention of Trengrouse's Rocket Life Saving Apparatus. Over the past two centuries, lighthouses, improvements to navigational aids and, more recently, advances in communications, sonar and radar have also helped to make the sea a safer place, bringing home to us all how things have changed and consigning the tragedy of shipwrecks, by and large, to history.

THE AGE OF SAIL
1527 - 1798

The seven shipwreck incidents in this section range from galleons, through Royal Navy men-o'-war, to a Falmouth Packet brig, but they all have one thing in common: their main form of propulsion was sail. During the age of exploration, with Columbus completing four round-trip voyages from Spain to the Americas between 1492 and 1503, the Portuguese explorer Vasco da Gama becoming the first European to reach India by sea in 1498, and several circumnavigations of the world during the 16th century, including Sir Francis Drake in the *Golden Hind* between 1577 and 1580, there were great advances in ship design. From cogs (medieval trading ships with a single mast and single square-rigged sail), the progression moved on through caravels (fast Portuguese ships with lateen sails which enabled them to sail close to the wind) and carracks (ocean-going ships with three or four masts, combining square- and lateen-rigs), to the famous galleons of the 16th century and finally galleasses, which were warships propelled by both sail and oars.

The three earliest ships featured here – the King of Portugal's treasure ship *St Anthony* (pages 14 to 19), lost in 1527; the Genoese galleon *Santo Christo de Castello* (pages 20 to 25), whose sinking in 1667 was eventually identified after much painstaking research; and the Dutch fluyt *Schiedam* (pages 26 to 31), wrecked off the Lizard in 1684 – were each built along 'modern' lines to adapt them to the great expansion in trade between Europe and the Far East. By the 17th century, the vessels were capable of carrying from 100 to 250 tons of cargo. As ships grew ever bigger so iron cannon replaced bronze, and their high poop and quarter decks were now streamlined to almost flush decks.

The Royal Navy's flagship HMS *Association* (pages 32 to 37), together with five other ships in the same fleet which blundered into the Western Rocks, Isles of Scilly, in poor visibility in 1707, was wrecked due to the inability to determine Longitude. Fourteen years later, another man-o'-war, HMS *Royal Anne* (pages 38 to 43), also made navigational errors, causing her to be driven onto the Lizard. The Falmouth Packet brig *Hanover* (pages 44 to 49) was not a warship but the illegal cargo of weapons and iron cannon which she was carrying made her heavier and less manoeuvrable. She fell victim to the weather, as did the Royal Navy's third-rate HMS *Colossus* (pages 50 to 55) when she sank off the Isles of Scilly in 1798, taking with her to the sea-bed Sir William Hamilton's priceless collection of antiquities as well as war loot taken from the French after the Battle of the Nile.

THE KING OF PORTUGAL'S TREASURE

PORTUGUESE GALLEON *St Anthony*

19 JANUARY 1527 – GUNWALLOE FISHING COVE, THE LIZARD

The main Lizard Road, on Thursday 19 January 1527, was packed with people from Helston and Mullion, all heading for Gunwalloe. The word on everyone's lips was 'shipwreck'. Anxious not to miss out, people cried 'Where is it?' 'Porth Lingey', a small cove near the Halzephron Inn where the men keep their fishing boats, was the response. Shipwrecks were nothing new to these Cornish folk, and from long experience they knew how to be prepared for one. The men carried long crowbars and Cornish shovels, the womenfolk brought empty wheat sacks and baskets, the children lengths of rope: everyone intent on plunder, should plunder be possible. Every walk of life was there, from local gentry in their horse-drawn carriages, to farmers with hay carts, longshore men from the Helford River, Cornish tin miners, inn keepers and labourers, to the down-and-outs; everyone looking to make a few shillings. This was a time when there were few laws governing shipwrecks and, if one could get away with it, it was a case of 'finders, keepers'. All manner of work ceased that day right across the Lizard peninsula, for the word was that this wreck was special – very special – since she belonged to a king!

That king was John III of Portugal and the ship, called the *St Anthony* (or, in its original Portuguese spelling, *Santo António*), was indeed his personal property, but she now lay on her beam ends on the shingle bank of Loe Bar, only a stone's throw out to sea. She was a large carrack, a sort of galleon, and the flagship of a fleet of eleven under the command of António Pacheco, returning to Lisbon from Flanders. The fleet had been on a trading voyage lasting three months and now, in the depths of winter, perhaps unwisely, they were returning home. Ten of the ships escaped the storm in the English Channel, but on 18 January 1527 the flagship, carrying a king's ransom in precious goods, was blown into Mount's Bay where she was wrecked. She lay at anchor all that night but at 8 a.m. the following morning, her anchor cables parted and she drove ashore at high tide at the far eastern end of Loe Bay, under Halzephron cliffs. Here there is a tiny cove, known today as Gunwalloe Fishing Cove but in 1527 as Porth Lingey, and it was there that the *St Anthony* was lost.

The agent for the Portuguese king in Amsterdam, Rui

Fernandes, the monarch's Treasurer, had instructed his assistant and secretary Francisco Pessoa, to carefully list the cargo loaded into the *St Anthony* before she sailed, it being so important and valuable. A copy of this manifest was given to the vessel's supercargo or overseer on board, Diogo Alvares, and was presumably lost in the wreck (although Alvares himself survived), but when Henry VIII's Court of Star Chamber was set up in London that October to investigate the wreck, the original Amsterdam inventory was sent by messenger to England, revealing exactly what the ship carried (see transcript on facing page). The values converted into sterling were written against each item on the Star Chamber inventory but the original spelling of several words has been changed for clarity.

The *St Anthony* was a ship of some 350 tons, carrying a crew of 86 of which 45 survived. In order to bring a case to the English Court of Star Chamber seeking restitution of the goods stolen by the defendants, the Portuguese survivors had to prove not only that violence had been used against them by the Cornish wreckers, but also that wholesale looting had taken place. The testimony of various members of the crew in court gives a flavour of what happened at Porth Lingey that day and for several days after.

'By reason of the great and urgent tempest of winds and weather and by the great outrages of the sea at Gunwalloe in the county of Cornwall, was perished and drowned in the sea there, many of the mariners and other persons then being within the same ship. And by great difficulty and danger to life forty-five of the persons which also were in the ship escaped and were saved and came to land

at about 8 of the clock in the forenoon of the same day. Which persons so saved with various others of the King's subjects those inhabited near there, with great pain, labour and difficulty, all that day and the next and the day following, endeavoured themselves to save and get out of the sea the goods to the use of the owners thereof.

During which time many of those persons which so laboured for the saving of the goods were thereby put in great jeopardy and danger of their lives, and one of them, being an inhabitant of Cornwall, was piteously drowned and perished.'

So far there is no mention of violence or intimidation. However, the testimony to the Court of Star Chamber goes on to record the actions of certain Cornish gentlemen, some of high rank:

'The Portuguese that came alive to land with the help of good men of the country saved on Saturday afternoon, as much goods as did amount to 1,000 ducats (£470) [£329,000 in 2018 values] and above. And so the good people of the country brought the goods to the Portuguese who did well reward and recompense them for their labours and pains taken, and so they continued in saving till night. The said night there came John Wylliam, miller and servant to Lord Godolphin, and two servants of Militon, one named Trehanneck the other Geyge, with their swords drawn and their shields in their hands, fell upon the Portuguese who were saving of their master's goods. The above three named persons with many other in their company took and spoiled from the Portuguese in their masters' name what it pleased them.

'Goods and Merchandise being in the King of Portugal's ship which perished on the coast of Cornwall'

In 8 thousand cakes or pieces of copper which cost	£3,234
Eighteen cakes or blocks of silver bullion which cost	£2,250
Three collections of silver vessels, basins, ewers, pots, bowls and other plate, and a chest with ready money	£3,576
Precious stones, pearls, chains, brooches and other jewels of gold	£2,664
In rich cloth of Arras tapestry and other rich hanging	£766
In cotton, Holland cloth and other linen cloth	£610
In satins, velvets and other silks	£400
In camlets, stays, and Satin of Bruges	£250
In frizados and Flemish cloth	£520
In fine English cloth of all manner of colours	£916
In English cottons and linings	£255
In 2,100 barbers' basins[1]	£164
In 3,200 latten (brass) candlesticks	£418
Six barrels of stopper nails	£40
A barrel of padlocks and weights	£20
Two barrels of packthread, needles and compasses	£50
A great chest of shawms and other instruments of music	£30
Four sered [sic] pipes, four complete harnesses for the King of Portugal's own person, and harnesses to his horses	£210
In pitch, tar, tallow and wainscot	£37
Brass guns, iron pieces and other artillery with the ship, and all other things belonging unto her	£2,470
Sum totals	£18,880[2]

[1] The barbers' basins would have been porcelain bleeding bowls

[2] To put that sum into perspective, a table of relative worth of that sum in 2019 would be between £6 and £12 million!

PORTUGUESE GALLEON *ST ANTHONY*

On the morrow, being Sunday, there came to the Portuguese Chynoweth and in his company one James Beauchamp, that could speak the language of Portugal, and required and inveigled the Portuguese to make sale of the ship, goods and merchandise. The Portuguese answered and said that "The ship and goods were all the King of Portugal's and so it doth appear upon our charter, whereof there is no man left alive that hath power to make sale thereof." Then the Portuguese made their complaint unto Chynoweth how they were robbed and spoiled on the night past and desired his council.'

James Chynoweth, a gentleman and constable of Marazion, and 'Officer for Wreck' to Arundel, offered to take Diogo Alvares, the Supercargo of the ship, along with one other Portuguese officer to meet three Justices of the Peace – Thomas St Aubyn of Clowance, William Godolphin of Breage and John Militon of Pengersick –

'that can give orders to have your goods returned to you'.

There Alvares repeated his complaint but was told:

'There is no remedy therein for it is the custom of the county regarding shipwreck goods, and if you and your fellows wilt sell unto us the ship and goods we will give you well therefore and will do the best for you that lies in our power.'

Although as the King's agent on board, Alvares had the authority to sell the King's property, he refused to do so. He then returned to a hamlet called Chinals, half a mile north of Halzephron, where they were lodged in John Chinal's house. Later that Sunday Richard Borno and a man named Lower, both Godolphin servants, John Polgrene, a servant of John Vivian, and several other men sent by St Aubyn appeared with drawn swords, broke into John Chinal's house and took away as much as they could carry. This must have been a frightening experience for the shipwrecked sailors, but there was more violence to come.

On the Monday following the wreck, the same men appeared again and demanded that Alvares sell them the wreck and any remaining cargo. In fear of their lives, a sale was agreed under duress for the sum of 1,000 ducats, plus 110 ducats for any cargo not yet recovered. Having got what they wanted, St Aubyn and the other Cornish gentlemen then took Alvares back to Clowance House where he was kept a prisoner, frequently being taken on horseback around Cornwall as some sort of trophy. When they heard of any wreck goods from the *St Anthony* in private hands, they confiscated them in the name of the King of Portugal, using Alvares as their authority. The remainder of the crew, now lodging in Treneves House in Helston, were having dinner when St Aubyn's men entered and stripped the Portuguese of any valuables they had, leaving them only their clothing.

The version of events offered by the defendants – St Aubyn, Godolphin and Militon – later at the court hearing was somewhat different. According to them:

'And on the morrow following, Alvares and his company, being in utter despair with no hope and trust for the saving and recovering

of the ship or any more of the goods they at any time had saved, and being such a number of Portuguese and having little money to maintain or bear their charges of meat and drink and other necessaries and to convey them home again to their own country, Alvares by agreement of the master of the ship and of Jeremy de Corfe, one of the gentlemen on board the St Anthony, the third day following the wreck moved Godolphin and Militon to buy from them parcels of goods which they then had saved amounting to the value of £20, also the ship's tackle and ordnance and all the residue of the goods which were at that time in the sea not recovered nor saved.'

The survivors returned to Lisbon, reported to the king, and the Amsterdam agent sent people to Cornwall to recover the cargo, but was denied access on the grounds that he did not bring with him proof that the goods belonged to the king. This gave King Henry VIII reason to appoint a Commission of Enquiry on 12 May 1527, culminating in everyone involved being ordered to attend a Court of the Star Chamber, the highest legal authority in England.

In the aftermath of the wreck, John Nicholas of Gunwalloe had made grapnels for the salvage of bronze cannon lying one fathom deep at low water (6 feet/2 metres), which Sir John Arundell promptly sold to Pendennis Castle. A local man, John Engofe, also found a silver gilt cross but Godolphin took that off him as well. A total of 1,534 of the copper ingots were recovered, barbers' basins, an iron cross-bow: all of course seized. Many years after the wreck seven cast iron cannon were recovered but again were seized by Arundell, using his authority as Vice Admiral of the West. Whilst the Cornish gentlemen defendants lost their court case, all three went on to become High Sheriffs of Cornwall, Godolphin was knighted and later Militon became Governor of St Michael's Mount. This is certainly the best-documented and most authentic account of what could happen to shipwreck goods in earlier times.

What remains of the *St Anthony* today.

The seabed where the *St Anthony* lies is now a protected wreck site. Despite the abundance of contemporary testimony, the exact site of the wreck was only discovered late into the 20th century. A copper ingot was fished up in the 1970s by a local shellfish diver, but the significance of the find was not recognised until later, when in 1981 a circular bun-shaped copper ingot was found by a holiday-maker on the foreshore. The team sent to investigate found that the location matched earlier accounts, so the decision was taken to dive the area. Using an underwater metal detector, 50 copper ingots were uncovered, as well as broken candlesticks, glass and pieces of lead, all items inventoried in the ship's manifest. Due to the rocky and shifting seabed, none of the ship's timbers nor any of the ferrous artefacts have survived, but other objects recovered can be seen in various locations. The Charlestown Shipwreck Centre has a display of *St Anthony* material, as does Pengersick Castle at Praa Sands. One of the divers later found a solid silver 'melon' or 'cake of silver' weighing 17 lbs (7.7 kg), one of the 18 listed in the manifest. This was sold to the British Museum for £3,500, after replicas were made.

19

THE 'MULLION PIN' WRECK
GENOESE GALLEON
Santo Christo de Castello

7 OCTOBER 1667 – NEAR MULLION, THE LIZARD

The late 16th and 17th centuries were the era of Great Discoveries, when horizons were being expanded, nations were creating new colonies and boundaries, ships were now trading around the world, and the old order was being challenged. A prime example was the increase in the use of ships to replace the traditional overland Silk Road trade routes from China and India into Europe, leading to the creation of the East India Companies by Portugal, the Netherlands, England, France and Sweden. East India Company ships could now bring home hundreds of tons of valuable commodities which were hitherto carried in much smaller quantities by pack animals on long and hazardous journeys across eight different countries to reach Europe. In addition to many different spices, silk, cotton, dyes, wood, ivory, pearls, rattan, tea and much more were all in great demand.

The most prominent European traders with the Far East were the Dutch who dominated this market from the late 1500s through to the 1790s. Warehouses in Amsterdam and London bulged with trade goods, the likes of which

few Europeans had seen. The East India ships brought home the goods, discharged them, sold them at auction to middle men, then set about another 12-month voyage back out to the Far East to buy more cargo. The distribution was left to smaller private vessels, one such ship being the Genoese 800-ton *Santo Christo de Castello*, which carried goods brought to the Netherlands from the Far East. The *Santo Christo de Castello* was an incredibly wealthy shipwreck by any standard; her cargo, which was worth £100,000 when she sank near Mullion in 1667, would today be the equivalent of £3 billion sterling!

Shipwrecks around Cornwall were legion but unpredictable, an important part of the economy for local Lords of the Manor for whom wrecks were a valuable perk as well as for the wrecking community of Cornwall. It is important to note that whilst earlier wrecks of lesser value were recorded and well known around Mullion, no mention of the *Santo Christo de Castello* existed in local lists, records or publications until her accidental discovery by a diver in 1969. Even then she remained an unidentified wreck site for a further four years before extensive and painstaking research finally revealed her name, her nationality and relevant details.

The wreck site was found early in 1969 by Peter McBride, a Logistics Sub-Lieutenant in the Royal Navy. Based at HMS *Seahawk*, the Royal Naval Air Station at Culdrose on the Lizard peninsula, Peter lived with his wife Bridget in Mullion village. He had only recently been transferred from RNAS Brawdy, in Pembrokeshire, and as a keen sports diver was interested in exploring this part of Cornwall's coast. In May 1969, assisted by Bridget, he carried his diving equipment down the steep path into the miniscule Polurrian Cove, put on his wetsuit and swam out to Angrouse Cliffs. Within minutes he had established two things: first, that there appeared to be some two dozen long iron objects on the seabed at a depth of 30 feet (9 metres), which suggested cannon but bore no resemblance to any cannon he had seen before. The second thing was not good news – the site lay directly beneath the main sewage outfall serving Mullion village, so that the sea was heavily polluted with unmentionables!

Back home in Peg-ne-Kay, Peter pondered over the iron objects he had seen, but came to no conclusion and after a few days, he consulted the author, who now takes up the tale:

'At the time I was a Chief Petty Officer Mechanician/Diver in the Torpedo Trials Unit and also ran the Air Station's sub-aqua club. Though we had never met before, we got on well and Peter told me of his find, inviting me to dive with him on the site some time. We dived together on 2 June and I was immediately attracted to the silvery glint of what appeared to be an almost buried coin on its edge. I dug it out to find it was a large silver medallion. Later, after cleaning, it proved to be a commemorative coronation medallion of Ferdinand IV, King of Bohemia, Hungary and Croatia, who was crowned as King of the Romans in 1653 (but died the following year before he could be elected as Holy Roman Emperor). What a remarkably lucky find that was, discovered on the first of hundreds of dives we made together on the site over the following years.'

The outstanding feature of the wreck was the many thousands of brass domestic pins scattered across the site, which were in six lengths from 1 to 4 inches (2 to 10 cms), and which pierced the divers' wetsuits and stuck into their knees and hands. For want of a better name the site was at first called 'the Mullion Pin Wreck', but after finding the medallion the name was changed to 'the Ferdinand'. The iron objects that Peter couldn't identify were in fact some 21 cannon, so abraded by seabed shingle washing over them for 300 years that their top halves had been completely worn away, leaving only their bottom halves and a shallow trough, the remains of the barrel tube. In fact, one gun even had a cannon ball still sitting in the remains of the bore at the breech end!

Despite the discovery of some remarkable artefact material, the ship's identity remained a mystery. It took three years of intensive research, scouring the records of the Royal Institution of Cornwall Library and the Cornish Studies Library without success, before the discovery of the Calendars of State Papers, Domestic Series, in

Plymouth Records Office provided the first clues to the name of this unidentified wreck and when she sank. The Calendars of State Papers date from Queen Victoria's time and comprise printed bound volumes containing a vast collection of transcribed, catalogued and indexed government documents going back to the 1300s, which had been rescued from certain decay in Whitehall cellars and storerooms and re-assembled in accessible form. The ship could not have sunk any earlier than 1653, the date on the medallion, so that was used as a starting point until, thousands of pages later, moving on to the Calendars of Spanish and Treasury State Papers, the year 1667 was reached – and bingo, there it was:

'7 October 1667 – Frances Bellot to Williamson, Pendennis. A Genoese [ship] richly laden and bound from London, after being two days at anchor, was at last cast upon the rocks, and broken to pieces.'

'9 October 1667 – Thomas Holden to James Hicks. The 5th instant there was cast away near the Lizard the Santo Christo de Castello, of 56 guns and about 500 tons. A new ship built at Amsterdam and come from thence laden with iron, lead, clothes and spices, to the value of £100,000, and 25 men and women drowned.'

At last there was a name that seemed to fit the wreck, but with no mention of Mullion, and the fact the wreck was 'cast away near the Lizard', there was no positive proof, so the search continued. Surely some documentation of such a rich vessel would have survived in local manor records?

It was then found that there were letters of the period all right, hundreds of them, especially regarding a ship called the *San Salvador*, lost in 1669, which muddied the waters. The 'Mullion Pin' wreck lay on Meres Ledges, land once belonging to Predannack Manor, but the Right of Wreck there belonged to the ancient Winnianton Manor which, using the original style and spelling:

'Tyme out of mynde and beyonde the memory of man extended and doe extende at thus presente from Carraglowes rock in the Parishe of Mullion in the County of Cornwall and to a place called Torvalloe articled by the sea coaste and soe far owt into the sea from any part of the lande within the said limits as a man can see a hamborough barrel from any part of the lande of the said manor.'

During most of the 16th century, Winnianton Manor was owned by the powerful Arundell family of Lanherne, which also held title to most of the hundred of Penwith and the Manor of Connerton. The Right of Wreck was an important source of income in those days, and Sir John Arundell claimed extensive rights of wreck in west Cornwall, the income from which normally amounted to half the value of any goods recovered. With the Lizard being a natural hazard to shipping, in 1624 it was proposed that a lighthouse be built on Lizard Point to help reduce shipwrecks. Sir William Monson, an infamous privateering captain, wrote in support:

'Mr Cavendish endured more hazard in a storm off the Lizard than in circumnavigating the globe.'

Having established the bounds of the manor in which the wreck lay, local sources were searched for the Court Rolls of Winnianton Manor and neighbouring Predannack. This showed that the *San Salvador*, wrecked locally, was carrying timber and provisions for the French fleet at Le Havre, and the Winnianton Rolls made mention of this and other wrecks:

'26 May 1670 – 'Warrant to Alderman William Bucknell and other farmers of the duty of five shillings a ton imposed on the French vessels in which Sieur Kerguelin Thomas has come over in order to take back the wreck of the Salvador, cast away upon the Lizard, which is to be restored to the French King.'

'1685 - Two anchors found on Growse Sands in Mullion Parish. Six guns salvaged.'

'1718 – The homage presents a flotant wrack of wine that happened on Meres tenement, that the 15th of such wracks doth belong to the Lord of the Manor. Wine and tar ashore, a cask of wine about 40 gallons, ashore at Porth Mellin.'

But it was the Calendar of State Papers, Domestic Series, for 1667 (29/219/127) that provided the crucial information. Transposed into modern spelling, it read:

'In August 1666, Giovanni Lorenzo Viviano, a rich Genoese, petitioned King Charles II for a passport for a newly-built ship, the Santo Christo de Castello. The ship (built in Amsterdam) was to proceed on a trading voyage from Amsterdam to Genoa, calling at the ports of London, Lisbon, Cadiz and other parts of Spain. The ship was fitted out at the expense of Genoese merchants resident in Genoa, and was to carry 48 guns and 120 seamen.'

The petition was obviously granted, since on 15 September 1667 she arrived at Falmouth (at this time another account describes her cargo as lead) with passengers for Tangier, the vessel having already called at London.

The actual date she left Falmouth is not known, but on 7 October, after lying at anchor on the west side of the Lizard, she was driven ashore near Mullion during a violent gale. Her captain and crew got ashore using the ship's boats, but 25 men and women passengers met their death by drowning. The same gale also put a Dutch flyboat of 15 tons, as well as a Spanish vessel, on the rocks at the Lizard, from which there were no survivors. On 3 December following the Mullion wreck, an Admiralty Commissioner sat at Falmouth on behalf of the proprietors, to examine all persons who had saved goods from the *Santo Christo de Castello*. No documentation of that event has been found, but incredibly a full transcript relating to the salvage of the wreck was found in the National Archives:

'William Painter of Sithney in the County of Cornwall, gent, maketh oath, that in the month of October 1667, particularly about the fifth day of the said month, a certain ship named the Santo Christo de Castello was split to pieces and cast away near Mullion to the westward of the Lizard, and many of her company were lost, but one Lorenzo Viviano who was Commander or Master of the said ship and some others who did belong to her came ashore and endeavoured to save what they could to carry

away with them or to dispose of the same. But they stayed there not long, the said Commander going from thence within two or three days and most of the company a month at most; and after they had disposed of such cinnamon, cloves and coral which was saved whilst they stayed there they forsook and left all the rest.

And since their departure a quantity of iron and lead and some guns, cables and an anchor have been recovered out of the sea, and some cinnamon, some Russian hides, and pieces of the ship, as masts and beams and other furniture thereunto belonging, have been also saved and have ever since being about the space of seventeen months been in the hands of Francis Godolphin Esquire or some parties by him entrusted to preserve the same, and some also in hands of other persons who have not yet delivered it into the custody of the said Vice Admiral, and the charge of keeping the same for warehouse room and looking to it doth daily increase, and the cinnamon and hides are grown worse and deteriorated by their long lying undisposed of.'

As far as is known, no other ship of this armament or tonnage remains unaccounted for in the area, and it is unlikely another wreck of this size and wealth would have escaped documentation. The silver coronation medallion of Ferdinand IV and the distinctly Dutch nature of artefacts recovered – candlesticks, a copper coin of 'Wes Friezlan' (West Friesland), tobacco boxes, religious figures, brass pins and miniature (5 ins/12 cms) 'time-gun' dial cannons – supported this as being the *Santo Christo de Castello*.

Proof that the original wreck was indeed very rich and valuable was supported by the quantity and range of artefacts the divers recovered. Boat-shaped lead ingots of 290 lbs (91.5 kgs), iron nails, brass domestic pins, thimbles, brass tobacco boxes and clay pipes bearing the makers initials 'EB'. The lid of one tobacco box was engraved with an image of Niewe Kerk tower, Delft (built only three years prior to the wreck), another with the Prince of Orange on horseback, a third with a biblical image of Tobias and the Angel from the Apocrypha. There were an enormous number of ornate brass furniture fittings and attachments, but the most spectacular and valuable find was Peter McBride's 'Tobacco Boy'. This was a bronze statuette of a nude male negro figure nearly 6 ins (15 cms) tall, its right arm holding a roll or twist of tobacco leaves, its raised left hand fitted with a small hole. Later a brass replica 'churchwarden' pipe (4.3 ins/11 cms) long was found, remarkably buried beneath a one-ton cannon some distance away, which fitted the hole in the statuette's left hand perfectly. This figure was a rare and valuable 17th century tobacco shop counter display, advertising the benefits of smoking.

What remains of the *Santo Christo de Castello* today?
Eroded cannon still mark the underwater site of the wreck, and almost all of the finds are now on display in the Charlestown Shipwreck Centre. The story of the wreck site was published in the International Journal of Nautical Archaeology (IJNA), Vol 3, No. 1, March 1974 and Vol 4, No. 2, Sept 1975. Conditions at the site were made worse when the sewer discharge pipe was replaced by one larger in diameter. Thankfully, with improved pollution laws, raw sewage is no longer pumped into the sea.

CAPTURED BY PIRATES
DUTCH FLUYT *Schiedam*

4 APRIL 1684 – NEAR GUNWALLOE CHURCH, THE LIZARD

Most shallow shipwreck finds are made by amateur sport divers, who often choose a headland, rock or cove where a ship might have come to grief, and then search the area thoroughly. They may simply swim the seabed and see what's there, or possibly tow a magnetometer behind their boat, an electronic device consisting of a towed 'fish', filled with special coil windings connected by a cable to an on-board electronic display unit. Magnetometers, developed in the 1980s for small boat work, work on the principle that they detect the difference between the earth's standing magnetic field and any non-ferrous metal on the seabed distorting the natural field. This could be cannon, anchors and chain, wire or steel plating, or simply an empty abandoned 40-gallon oil drum!

When British Telecom engineer Tony Randall decided to explore the cove known as Jangye Ryn or Dollar Cove, to the west of Gunwalloe Church on the Lizard Peninsula, in 1971, the portable magnetometer was not an option, since it was still in its infancy and very expensive to buy. Tony therefore donned his wetsuit and diving gear on the beach, swam out into deeper water and commenced a zig-zag swim search in 30 feet (10 metres) just to see what was out there, if anything. To his astonishment, within minutes he was looking at nine huge iron cannon and evidence of a large number of other iron objects, intermixed with various small brass and copper items part buried in the seabed. Additional exploration revealed 19 cannon in total, all 24-pounders, so had he discovered a long-forgotten warship wreck? There was no recorded man-o'-war lost in that area and no merchant vessel would be so heavily armed, so what was this shipwreck? It took Tony and his team (of which the author was a member) almost ten years of diving, exploration, research and general enquiries to establish its origin, history and story, which proved to be remarkable, involving Dutch traders, pirates, the Royal Navy and the Moroccan town of Tangier. Nature frequently buried the site under several feet of sand, then following a gale it would uncover again, so that exploration over that period was both unpredictable and spasmodic.

The ship proved to be the *Great Schiedam* of Hoorn or, as the

Dutch recorded her, the *Groette Scherdam van Horn*, a typical dumpy wooden 400-ton fluyt, a cargo-carrying workhorse, a precursor to the English flyboat. Built for the Baltic timber trade, she sailed from Hoorn in late April 1683 bound for Ribadeo on the north coast of Spain where she loaded a cargo of timber. When close to Gibraltar on 1 August she was spotted by a Barbary Coast pirate frigate of 14 guns, which fired a warning shot as an order for her to stop. The pirate ship then went alongside, her crew of Corsair Moors swarming across the fluyt's upper deck, taking the crew prisoner. Having looted the ship of anything valuable, the pirates then herded the entire crew apart from the cook into their own ship, the Dutchmen under no illusion as to their fate: they were destined to become slaves. The two vessels then parted company, the frigate off to seek more prey, the *Great Schiedam* with a pirate crew heading for their base in Salé, on the Atlantic coast of Morocco, the Dutch cook catering for the 34 Moors on board.

Due to prevailing winds they were still at sea ten days later, only now the hunters had become the hunted since on the horizon had appeared the British sixth-rate HMS *James Galley*, commanded by Captain Clowdisley Shovell who at this stage of his career was engaged in the defence of Tangier against Salé raiders. Twenty-four years later, after receiving a knighthood and being promoted to Admiral of the Fleet, Sir Clowdisley was to lose his life when his flagship HMS *Association* sank in the Isles of Scilly in 1707 (see pages 32 to 37). Under full sail and with the advantage of 40 sweeps or oars giving her great manoeuvrability, she swept down on the lightly-armed four-gun fluyt whose pirate crew stood no

chance of escape. An extract from Captain Shovell's logbook gives some idea of what happened.

'10th August 1683 – A fresh Gale This morning about ½ an hour past five o' clock, we see a Sail Bearing NW x W and Steered after her. At 11 o' Clock we came up with her, it is a flyboat of 400 ton Called the Groette Scherdam van Horn; who had been from thence 3½ months and she had been at Ribadus [Ribadeo]; and delivered of Cable, Cordage and Anchors then loaded with Timber bound to Cadiz. The pirates on the first of this month did take her off the North Cape and had sent her towards Sallen's [Salé] with 34 Moors and one Dutchman that did belong to her, he being their Cook.'

All the Moors were taken on board the *James Galley* as prisoners, strip-searched for weapons, then herded onto the gun deck under the watchful eyes of armed Royal Marines. Some 30 Royal Navy sailors took the place of the pirates as crew and sailed the *Great Schiedam* to Cadiz, where they sought a market for her cargo of timber as a prize. By a remarkable coincidence, the frigate HMS *Sapphire* then entered port, announcing she had just chased, run ashore and destroyed a 14-gun Moorish frigate, the vessel that had captured the *Great Schiedam*! The owner of the timber cargo then appeared, having travelled overland from Ribadeo, and was prepared to buy it back, but before a settlement could be reached the Admiralty ordered both the *James Galley* and the *Great Schiedam* to cross the Straits and dock in Tangier.

Tangier at the time was an English stronghold, passed to

King Charles II in 1661 as part of the marriage dowry of his Queen, Catherine of Braganza, and had since been the subject of enormous Government expenditure in materials and manpower, turning a small undefended port into a fortress. Having this base at the entrance to the Mediterranean gave England unprecedented naval influence in the area to enforce her foreign policies. To protect the fleet from Atlantic gales, a huge mole or breakwater had been constructed under the guidance of Sir Hugh Cholmley, assisted by the finest of England's civil engineers. By the time it was completed it had absorbed 167,000 tons of stone, stretched a quarter of a mile (500 metres) out into the sea, with a top surface road 18 feet (5 metres) above high water. It had cost over £1 million, plus the costs of the actual Garrison.

No sooner had the *Great Schiedam* and the frigate *James Galley* entered Tangier harbour than they received orders to return to Cadiz, in order that her timber cargo could be sold. The Admiralty wanted to make use of this additional vessel, but with her hold still full of timber she was a liability. A sale took place, the owner was seemingly satisfied, so now the *Great Schiedam* could begin a new career as a water-carrier. Despite all the expenditure on Tangier's defences, a basic public supply of fresh water had been sadly neglected, so for several weeks the *Great Schiedam* and her escort sailed back and forth carrying barrels of drinking water.

On 17 September 1683 a British fleet entered Tangier, carrying Admiral of the Fleet Lord Dartmouth, who immediately assumed command of the town from Colonel Percy Kirke. Lord Dartmouth was accompanied by Samuel Pepys, who wrote an account of the evacuation. They broke the news that Great Britain was giving up Tangier, that the town was to be destroyed and the mole blown up. The reason for this was that the port had become indefensible, being overlooked by high ground occupied by Moors, and was now too expensive to maintain. First, all the properties in the town had to be valued for compensation before being blown up, an operation that occupied five months, whilst at the same time the Garrison was slowly reduced.

The *Great Schiedam* was then relieved of her water-carrying duties, and under the command of Captain Gregory Fish was allocated a full crew of English officers and seamen, so that she could make passage for Portsmouth carrying army stores. The fortifications on the mole itself were stripped of cannon, and their iron 24- and 32-pounder guns loaded in the fluyt's hold, carefully placed muzzle to breech or 'top to tail', with lots of timber dunnage to stop them moving whilst at sea. Whatever other items the military wanted to save were taken on board – garrison gun carriages and wheels, gun limbers, shot, shell and tools, plus a company of miners and their families, horses and machinery. She left Tangier for the last time on 26 February 1684, carrying a complement of 120 men, women and children, a huge number for such a small vessel, and it is certain that she was grossly overloaded. Captain Fish's orders were to sail in convoy along with a hospital ship, several merchant vessels, various prize ships and an armed escort, the third-rate HMS *Montagu*, captained by Henry Killigrew. At the last minute, Lord Dartmouth changed his mind and substituted the fourth-rate man-o'-war HMS *Oxford*, under Captain John Tyrrell, for the *Montagu*.

That the *Great Schiedam* carried a large number of crew and passengers is borne out by a letter from Lord Dartmouth, addressed to 'the Comptroller of Victualling of His Majestie's Navy' at Tangier:

> '– and you are also to cause to be put aboard His Majesties flyboat ye Schiedam, Mr Gregory Fish Commander, a proportion of victuals for 125 men for 42 days to enable him to transport to England the workmen and other people lately belonging to the Mole here. For which this shall be your warrant. Dated at Tangier, 30th day of January 1684.'

The homeward-bound fleet now consisted of the *Great Schiedam*; the ketch *Deptford*; the yacht *Ann*; two prize vessels, the *Swan* and the *Two Lyons*; also the hospital ship *Welcome* and the *Charles*. Beset by winter gales the convoy soon became scattered, and it was the beginning of April before they were comfortably together and into the English Channel. Unfortunately, Captain Fish was convinced his ship was still off the coast of France and not within Mount's Bay. The *Great Schiedam* drove ashore at Gunwalloe on 4 April, going aground in the shallows only some 200 yards offshore at 4 a.m. There was no recorded loss of life amongst the 120 on board, but a number of horses were sacrificed, since it is recorded that the captain was not prepared to pay for their rescue. The survivors saved by the locals were then taken by horse and cart to Falmouth, some 12 miles away, and put on board HMS *Montagu* which had arrived from Tangier en route to Portsmouth.

Lord Dartmouth was at anchor in the Downs when he heard of the wreck and thought it due to the incompetence of Captain Fish, probably influenced in his opinion by a letter he received a few days later from Colonel Kirke of Pendennis Castle, who reported that

> 'Mr Fish lies abed and cries instead of saving the wreck, and if he would have promised the country people to pay them they would have saved the horses, for they stood but up to the belly in water for six hours, in short he is a greater beast than any of them…'

This accounts for the issue of a warrant for his arrest and trial by William Joynes, General Marshall of the High Court of Admiralty, but Fish appears to have been acquitted by a court-martial from any blame for the loss of the *Schiedam*. With the wreck in shallow water, the Admiralty appointed a Richard Sampson of Helston as the salvage master. The anchors, guns and heavy equipment recovered were taken by sea to Gweek, near Helston, at the head of the Helford Estuary, then shipped to Portsmouth. Rigging, sails, cordage and items generally spoilt by the sea were sold off locally but there was a huge financial loss due to pilfering. Even Richard Sampson, who had estimated he would make a profit when accepting the salvage contract, failed to raise half the amount he expected.

The fact that there were still 19 iron cannon on the wreck site when it was first rediscovered suggests that salvage had proved difficult. The site is rock-strewn and very shallow, so

30

what boats were originally employed in the salvage is not known, but being wide open to the prevailing south-west wind must have made things difficult. Since 1971, as seabed conditions allowed and the depth of sand changed, several pewter plates have been recovered, one with a clear but still unidentified crest. Other finds include hand tools, lead boxes, a complete 'nest' of copper cooking pots and vessels inside of which were neatly coiled copper barrel hoops, suggesting they were from military gunpowder barrels. An unusual aspect of the wreck site was an abundance of ornate hand-carved marble sections, as if someone in Tangier had sent home a large dismantled marble fireplace or similar. Whilst dozens of pieces were recovered, they did not fit any general pattern so it is unlikely that their original function or purpose will ever be known.

What remains of the Great *Schiedam* today?

The site was granted Protected Wreck status in 1982 under the Protection of Wrecks Act 1973, which means that only licensed divers may visit the area. The copper cooking pot 'nest', barrel hoops, lead boxes and other items can be seen in the Charlestown Shipwreck Centre; the pewter plates, many personal items and the ship's rudder are on display at Pengersick Castle, Praa Sands, near Marazion in Cornwall. There was a display of artefacts in the Royal Institution of Cornwall Museum in River Street, Truro, for many years, and they may still have artefacts in their reserve collection. The wreck attracted TV and media coverage in early June 2018 when a diver reported the site was again uncovered, though this is in fact a frequent event.

A typical Dutch fluyt.

DUTCH FLUYT *SCHIEDAM*

THE LOSS OF SIR CLOWDISLEY SHOVELL'S FLAGSHIP
HMS *Association*

22 OCTOBER 1707 – WESTERN ROCKS, ISLES OF SCILLY

In the long history of the Royal Navy, two non-wartime incidents stand out, both for a tragic loss of ships and particularly for an unprecedented loss of men. Both occurred early in the 18th century, during the reign of Queen Anne, and remarkably the same man-o'-war and the same officer were involved each time. The first incident was the 'Great Storm' of 1703, whose epicentre was the Thames Estuary, the second the disaster of 1707 in the Isles of Scilly.

The 'Great Storm' which commenced on Thursday 26 November (according to the Old-Style Julian calendar; 7 December 1703 in the Gregorian calendar in use today), saw a fleet of seven warships lately returned from the Mediterranean at anchor in the Gunfleet, one of which was the *Association*, then the flagship of Sir Stafford Fairborne, Vice-Admiral of the Red. Another was the *Russell*, flagship of Admiral Sir Clowdisley Shovell, a rising star in Queen Anne's navy, which in the tempest lost all her anchors, her complete rudder and main mast, was driven by the wind to the Dutch coast where she grounded on soft mud and

was saved. The *Association* lost her rudder on the Gunfleet Sand and, unable to steer, was driven north all the way to Gothenburg in Sweden. The Admiralty had given up the *Association* as lost with all hands following the storm, so were greatly relieved when she limped back to Chatham having been missing completely for 48 days. Unfortunately, 13 other naval ships were wrecked and lost, including the entire Channel squadron, and the total loss of life around the nation was estimated at between 8,000 and 15,000 people, of whom over 1,500 were seamen.

In the summer of 1707 Sir Clowdisley Shovell, by now Admiral of the Fleet and as famous in his day as Admiral Lord Horatio Nelson became in his, arrived off Nice with a squadron of British warships along with Sir George Byng and Sir John Norris. Their orders were to co-operate with the Austrian Imperial Army under Prince Eugene of Savoy in bombarding and capturing the French port of Toulon. Britain wanted total command of the Mediterranean, and Toulon offered a base from which its fleet could operate all year round. Gibraltar as yet could offer neither full dockyard nor victualling facilities, which meant Royal Navy ships had to run the gauntlet of the weather returning from the Mediterranean to Britain each autumn, unable to stay at sea during the winter.

The allies failed to capture Toulon, but bombardment by Shovell's forces panicked the French into scuttling their own fleet. Sir Clowdisley and his ships withdrew to Gibraltar, where the fleet was split, some remaining there for the winter, others allocated to escort convoys, whilst the twenty-two ships that Sir Clowdisley was to bring back to Portsmouth were busy re-storing and victualling before heading for home. The fleet left Gibraltar on 30 September, Sir Clowdisley flying his pennant in the second-rate, 78-gun *Association*. By 5 October they were well out into the Atlantic, but already meeting strong head winds. The fleet was sailing abreast in three columns, seven ships in each, the flagship fourth from the head in the right-hand column led by the first-rate *Royal Anne*. By 20 October they were steering north-east with the wind astern, confident that the mouth of the English Channel lay just ahead. However, in 1707 navigation when out of sight of land was still rudimentary. A ship's position north and south on the globe (her latitude) was easily calculated, but her east or west position (longitude) was still an educated guess dictated by dead-reckoning. Hence the fleet knew when it was level with the English Channel but had no idea whether they were east or west of the Isles of Scilly, which presented a huge rock-strewn obstacle if they had got it wrong – which

they had. At about eight o'clock in the evening on 22 October 1707 (Old Style Julian calendar; 2 November by the modern calendar), in the dark, in bad visibility and a moderate gale, they blundered into the Western Rocks of the Isles of Scilly, close to where the Bishop Rock lighthouse stands today.

Here the flagship struck the Outer Gilstone rock and sank, with the loss of everyone on board, some 750 men. HMS *St George*, another second-rate, struck the same rock but though damaged, managed to get off, whilst both the third-rate HMS *Eagle* and the fourth-rate HMS *Romney* also sank nearby, with only one survivor between them. Two smaller fireships, *Phoenix* and *Firebrand*, were also in trouble having struck the rocks. The *Phoenix*, leaking badly, reached the channel between Bryher and Samson and managed to beach herself on Tresco's sandy foreshore in New Grimsby harbour, where she remained for three months undergoing repairs. The *Firebrand*, half-full of water, made her way towards St Agnes and the only lighthouse on the islands, entering Smith Sound only to sink near Menglow Rock in 10 fathoms with only 20 men saved out of 48.

From the Admiralty Neat (Pay) Books[1], now in the National Archives, which names every officer, Royal Marine and seaman on board a particular ship, giving his rank, daily pay and next of kin, it has been possible to establish that around 1,450 men died that night, not the 2,000 sometimes claimed. Four ships sank in total with only one survivor

[1] The *Association*'s Neat Book was started on 1 July 1704 and closed on the day she sank.

between them, quartermaster George Lawrence, who had been on board the *Romney*. He survived clinging to a rock for a whole day until rescued, that rock bearing his name to this day. The other 18 warships in the fleet all made it safely to Portsmouth. We can only imagine what the men on board those five ships that were lost suffered that night, with huge seas roaring across their decks slowly tearing the ships to pieces, the air filled with the screech of timbers being torn apart, the grinding of their hulls on rocks, the screaming wind, but above all the tormented cries of hundreds of men in their dying moments.

There are many legends surrounding the loss of the *Association* and Sir Clowdisley, but unfortunately all have been discredited. There was no meeting of captains to

'Mumper', Sir Clowdisley's dog.

discuss their location. It is highly improbable that the Admiral had a Scillonian seaman hanged for telling him he was too close to the islands. He was not murdered, neither was one of his fingers cut off by an old woman to steal an emerald ring. His body was in fact found on the foreshore at Porthellick, St Mary's, and later taken on board the man-o'-war HMS *Salisbury* to Plymouth's Citadel. Here he was embalmed, placed in a coffin and eventually buried at Queen Anne's personal expense in Westminster Abbey, a national hero. However, an unsolved mystery concerns the finding of Sir Clowdisley's body, together with those of his two stepsons, Sir John and James Narborough, his Flag-Captain Edmund Loades, the son of the Bishop of Winchester, and Shovell's pet greyhound Mumper, all in Porthellick Cove. Their combined presence in one place suggests they got there in a ship's boat, but what of the sailors who would have rowed it the seven miles from the Gilstone? And since they must have passed St Agnes island and its lighthouse which we know was lit that night, why did they not land there? We shall never know.

Captain Loades and Shovell's two stepsons were buried in the nave of Old Town church, Isles of Scilly, their graves left outside the building when it was reduced in size following the demolition of its eastern end. Another mystery is the lack of documentary evidence of the effect the 1707 disaster had on the islands. Owned by the Duchy of Cornwall, the steward would have informed his employer of the event; the commanding officer of the Garrison and Star Castle as well as locals, would surely have written letters about this momentous event, yet none have been found to date.

Bodies of drowned seamen must have turned up all round the islands for weeks after, and no doubt a mass burial grave was created, said to be the sports field on St Agnes, but even ground penetration radar there has to date failed to locate any soil disturbance. Unfortunately, all the church records for Scilly prior to 1726 were lost in a fire, so all we know is that the Reverend Henry Penneck, St Mary's chaplain,

'– went away the same year, 1707.'

Perhaps the stress and strain of having to officiate at the interment of so many corpses proved all too much for him?

As a direct result of the 1707 disaster, the government introduced a Longitude Act in July 1714, stating

'It is well known by all that are acquainted with the Art of Navigation, that nothing is so much wanted and desired at Sea as the discovery of Longitude, for the Safety and Quickness of Voyages and Preservation of Ships and the lives of Men.'

Three levels of financial prize were offered, the largest being £20,000 (£3 million in 2018), yet the winner, John Harrison, despite designing a nautical chronometer in 1730 which in trials proved to be entirely satisfactory regarding its accuracy and meeting all the conditions of the Act, never actually received the full amount or official recognition of his achievement.

The wreck sites of the lost ships of Sir Clowdisley's fleet were eventually located, appropriately by divers of the Royal Navy, in 1967 to 1969 after four annual expeditions. Five bronze cannon of French origin which had been captured at Vigo Bay, bronze signal guns, pewter dishes and silver cutlery, as well as personal artefacts and thousands of gold and silver coins were found and raised. Regrettably, although the Prime Minister Harold Wilson, who was on holiday on St Mary's at the time, ordered an extension of the Navy divers' presence, eventually they had to return to their service duties, leaving the wreck sites wide open to any civilian divers who wanted to exploit them. Even the Admiralty salvage contract awarded to the naval diving team before they found the *Association* was not worth the paper on which it was written, the Navy having later issued identical contracts to two civilian teams! Today, the *Association* and *Eagle* sites are Protected Wrecks, unfortunately 50 years too late, the stable doors having been shut long after the horse had bolted!

What remains of the 1707 wrecks today?

The wreck site of the *Association* around the Outer Gilstone still holds two anchors and scores of iron cannon in depths ranging from 15 feet (4.5 metres) down to 120 feet (36 metres). HMS *Eagle* lies on Tearing Ledge in a gully 115 feet (35 metres) deep, iron cannon spread along its length with anchors at one end. The site of the *Romney* is so far yet to be found and identified, although some say it lies near Old Bess rock. Though the *Firebrand* is still virtually pristine, the site is not protected as yet. She lies in some 60 feet (18 metres), close to Menglow Rock in Annet Sound, still holding all her original cannon and anchors, the only wreck of a fireship in UK waters. There are even a few original timbers surviving, unlike the other 1707 sites which have none remaining.

The bulk of the Navy finds ended up in museums. Of the five bronze cannon from the *Association*, one sits on a replica gun carriage in Tresco Gardens, another is in the Tower of London's Armoury collection, a third which was mounted outside a London Gun Club premises was stolen, and the other two were sold, though their location is unknown. The St Mary's Museum on Scilly has an extensive range of material from the *Association*, mostly donated by the Royal Navy, including a fine bronze 'land-gun' inscribed '*Charles of Devonia ordered this gun made by Thomas Pitt in the*

year 1604', no doubt one of Shovell's trophies of war. They also have the *Eagle*'s bell. Elsewhere there are hundreds of artefacts from all the sites in the Charlestown Shipwreck Centre, while the *Firebrand*'s bell is still in private hands on St Mary's. But with no wreck protection law in those days, finds by civilian divers mostly ended up in auction houses, private collections or on the divers' mantelpieces. Unfortunately, this means there is no overall inventory of what was recovered.

For further reading, Peter McBride and Richard Larn have published a definitive account of the 1707 wrecks in their book *Admiral Shovell's Treasure and Shipwreck in the Isles of Scilly* (Shipwreck & Marine, 1999).

The *Association* before the storm.

HMS *ASSOCIATION*

THE GHOSTS OF PISTOL MEADOW
HMS FRIGATE GALLEY *Royal Anne*

10 NOVEMBER 1721 – LIZARD POINT

In March 1709, when the Royal Dockyard at Woolwich launched the *Royal Anne*, she was the 17th such frigate-galley in the Royal Navy, an innovative and initially secret type of warship which had already proved their worth. Heavily-armed, carrying up to 42 bronze and iron cannon, in addition to conventional square sails on all three masts, frigate-galleys' secret weapon was their alternative form of propulsion. They could be rowed with up to 66 oars known as 'sweeps', which was a huge advantage over conventional sailing ships, especially in light wind conditions. The Navy built 25 of them between 1676 and 1782, to combat what became known as the Golden Age of Atlantic piracy. In 1719 alone, pirates took 34 ships between April and August, a number of which were destroyed by burning, their crews taken into slavery. Consequently, in response to political pressure and petitions by merchants and slave-traders, British warships were sent to combat them.

The *Royal Anne*, one of five frigate-galleys finished in 1709, was a two-decked vessel with very fine lines, most of her armament being on the upper deck. She was designed to row equally as efficiently as she could sail. This allowed her guns to be brought to bear whilst manoeuvring using her oars, regardless of the wind, which was a new tactic for the Royal Navy. The launch of the *Royal Anne* was recorded in *The London Journal*:

> '*Tuesday 30th June 1709 – was launched at Woolwich the Royal Anne Galley, of a new invention under the direction of the Marquis of Carmarthen, carrying 40 guns, being the finest that was ever built.*'

Technically she was a fifth-rate man-o'-war, carrying a crew of 247, weighing 511 tons, her gun deck 127 feet (38.7 metres) long, her beam 31 feet (9.5 metres). Her upper deck bulwarks were pierced for guns, whilst the lower deck had a line of smaller openings known as sweep ports to accommodate her oars. She could row 33 oars each side, 66 in total, and was allowed 60 extra crew to help man them. With three men to each oar they could propel the ship at 3 knots. Her first commission was convoy duty off Norway, protecting the Russian trade, then between Norway and

Yarmouth, which set a pattern for her 12-year career. It was not until 1719 that she was sent overseas to Guinea, Cape Verde and Africa, returning to Deptford in May 1721. She was then earmarked to take Lord Belhaven and his retinue to Barbados in the West Indies, which would require the creation of additional cabin space aft and on the sweep deck. Hence her armament of six-pounder guns was cut down, while her crew was also reduced to number only 185.

Unfortunately, on 12 September 1721, on her way from Chatham to Spithead in the Solent, where her important passengers for the West Indies were to embark, she went aground on the Brake Bank in the Downs, inside of the Goodwin Sands, then collided with the *Spolswood*, a Virginian merchant ship. Damage must have been slight, since she was able to leave Cawsand Bay, Plymouth, by the evening of 7 November, under the command of Captain Willis and with her important guest and 24 gentlemen passengers now on board.

The principal passenger was the 29-year old Douglas John Hamilton of Biel (in the Scottish county of Haddington), the third Lord Belhaven, who was to take up the Governorship of Barbados, allegedly to avoid the suspicion of having murdered his wife Anne, although no proof of this has been found. *The London Journal* mentions that

'Lord Belhaven's luggage, and the chief part of his servants, were sent to Barbados about two months ago.'

On 8 November they were abeam of Dodman Point, and

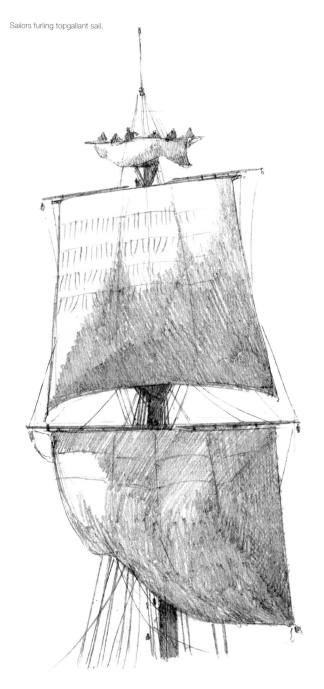

Sailors furling topgallant sail.

40

the following day at 4 p.m. saw land about five leagues off, which they took to be the Lizard. The wind was now WSW and blowing fresh. They tacked south again; then, as the wind increased, took down the fore topmast to reduce windage and lay to until midnight, when Captain Willis decided they should return to Plymouth. Unaware that in the dark that the wind and tide had set them close in to the Lizard, she steered north-east, and at about 3 a.m. struck a rock which was

'but a pistol shot from the coast of the Lizard.'

The *Royal Anne* bilged and in only 15 minutes started to go to pieces, her port side falling away, taking many men with it. The *Daily Post* of 27 November 1721 tells us that

'it is believed that about 300 persons lost their lives in this unfortunate accident.'

She had struck just south-west of the Lizard Point, close to the Quadrant Rock. In addition to her captain, all her officers, Lord Belhaven and the 24 'gentlemen passengers', 207 members of the crew drowned and there were only three survivors. These were Thomas Goodall, William James and Robert Wilson, presumably all seamen. On 17 November, the *Daily Post* had already reported that

'—all hands were set to work in their shirts to get her off the rock, but the second shock, which happened some minutes after the first, dashed her to pieces. The three survivors were saved by clinging to pieces of wreckage. Robert Wilson was on a plank with four

others who were washed off by the waves, but he saved himself by swimming to a rock where he stayed until the next morning.'

As will be seen in the chapter about HMS *Anson* (pages 58 to 63), The Burial of Drowned Persons Act of Parliament of 1808, also known as Grylls' Act after the local solicitor who drafted the new law, required that all the rites of Christian burial regardless of colour or creed should be observed regarding the bodies found on the foreshore, all at the expense of the local parish. However, there was no such lawful requirement in 1721, so the victims of the *Royal Anne* tragedy suffered the usual ignominy of a mass grave. The local inhabitants of the Lizard buried the 208 bodies found in individual pits in Pistol Meadow, a field overlooking the nearest cove to the wreck. Each pit is said to have contained some 10 to 30 bodies, and local legend has it that until the 1850s, the long irregular mounds surmounting the pits were still visible. The Reverend C. A. Johns, who wrote a book entitled *A Week at the Lizard* in 1848, makes mention of Pistol Meadow as being haunted. The name 'Pistol' has caused much speculation as to its origin, but is merely a corruption of 'Pistyll', the old Celtic name for a waterfall, and a small stream running through the meadow to the cliff edge does in fact create such a feature.

Five days after the wreck, the Admiralty instructed Captain Rowley of the vessel *Lively* to proceed from Plymouth to the Lizard to save what he could from the *Royal Anne*. In the public records there is a letter from Lizard fishermen dated 2 May 1722, concerning a 26 cwt (263 kg) anchor and 21 cannon salvaged. At least five other references to salvage are in the public domain which mention 20 guns from the *Royal Anne* at Pendennis Castle, Falmouth; also guns delivered to Flushing Quay. Twelve named individuals received £103.13s.6d between them for their efforts. Two vessels are named as having been sent from Portsmouth to work on the wreck: the *Jolly Bachelor* and the Royal Yacht *Henrietta*, which even arrived with a newly-invented diving machine 'to fish on the wreck'. This may well have been the copper Diving Engine, or bell, designed and put into practice just a year earlier by one of the pioneers of English diving, Captain Jacob Rowe. The salvage work brought a complaint from a George Robinson of damage caused to his estate.

The wreck of the *Royal Anne* then remained undisturbed until 1969, when eight cannon and iron and lead shot were discovered close to Taylor's Rock, near the Quadrant. Details of the site and its location were passed to the Bristol University Sub-Aqua Club which, over a period of four years, carried out an archaeological survey. They found pottery shards, lead and iron shot, a number of English silver coins dated between 1710 and 1720, but nothing that positively identified the site as being that of the *Royal Anne*. In 1991 the site was then rediscovered by Rob Sherratt, who surveyed and excavated the site with the assistance of Mike Hall who lives nearby on the Lizard, recovering some 400 artefacts. Their most significant find, in addition to English gold sovereigns of the period, included the handle of a silver spoon and other items of cutlery bearing Lord Belhaven's family crest, the only artefacts which gave the site a positive identification.

In 2004 Wessex Archaeology sent a team of divers to make an assessment of the site on behalf of English Heritage. Then between 2006 and 2014 CISMAS (Cornwall & Isles of Scilly Maritime Archaeological Society), led by Kevin Camidge of Penzance, carried out a Marine Environmental Assessment. Archaeological excavation work for the same authority produced four lengthy reports which can be found on the CISMAS website (www.cismas.org.uk). The nature of the *Royal Anne* site, the remains of the only known 18th-century frigate-galley in UK waters, justified all this attention and since 1993 the *Royal Anne* has been a Designated Wreck under the Protection of Wrecks Act (1973).

What remains of the *Royal Anne* today?

As a Designated Wreck, diving is prohibited without a licence. Two iron cannon remain on the site in a depth of 6 metres, and there are environmental dispersal trial objects on the seabed which should not be touched. The handle of the spoon bearing the crest of Lord Belhaven's family and other artefacts are now in the possession of the late Robert Sherratt's family.

Lizard Point.

HMS FRIGATE GALLEY *ROYAL ANNE*

SUNK CARRYING GOLD AND ILLEGAL WEAPONS PACKET BRIG *Hanover*

2 DECEMBER 1763 – HANOVER COVE, ST AGNES

The Falmouth Packet Service came about out of sheer necessity as the British Empire and its colonies continued to grow in the 18th century. From the English Royal Postal Service (initially an overland communication system started in 1654), a direct sea service to Spain commenced in 1688, with Falmouth being chosen as the terminal port for its secure harbour and easy access to sea routes both to the south and west. With the expansion of British colonies across the Atlantic and the growth in trade with the West Indies and Brazil as well as the Mediterranean, the mail service was forced to expand to meet demand. The Falmouth Packet Service quickly grew and prospered, its ships carrying private mail, diplomatic and government dispatches and army and navy communications; soon the service was expanded to include passengers, bullion and specie, particularly between banks.

The first Packet Agent appointed at Falmouth was in 1688, and the first regular service by sea was to La Coruña, although the outbreak of war with Spain in 1701 saw the service diverted to Lisbon. By 1800 the service was operating 39 packet ships out of Falmouth, employing 1,200 officers and men, as well as an army of shore-based clerks, store-keepers, agents, lawyers, bankers, clergy, dockers and labourers. In fact the Packet Service was the making of Falmouth. Those ships carried over 3,000 passengers each year, and in 1757 alone transported over £1.5 million in gold and silver.

There were five packet vessels altogether by the name of *Hanover*, each of which were privately-built and leased to the service by their owners, usually their captains. *Hanover* (1) was hired by the service for the Lisbon run at £75 a month until the late 1730s when she was replaced by a new ship *Hanover* (2). She was built in 1739 and reported to be of 160 tons, armed with 14 iron cannon and six swivel guns, the latter to deter possible pirate boarders. She carried a crew of 57 under Captain Philip Enouf, and the 1739 Post Office Establishment Book shows she was hired for £2,802.4s.1d per annum. Returning from Lisbon in April 1748 a privateer attempted to capture her, causing Captain Enouf to order his vessel be lightened in an attempt to escape. This resulted in six 3-pounder cannon and carriages being thrown overboard, plus one anchor, 600 feet of 11-inch (28-cm) cable, 50 feet of old rope and various stores, which increased her speed sufficiently for her to escape unscathed. Grateful that he had saved both the ship and the mail, the Post Office reimbursed her captain the sum of £112.9s.

Ownership of *Hanover* (2) then changed hands and Captain Joseph Sherburn took over from September 1755. On 6 March 1757 she was captured by the French privateer *Count de Bentem* of St Malo and carried to Brest. When eventually Captain Sherburn and his crew were released and returned to Falmouth, the Post Office compensated Sherburn with £3,064.1s.1d. *Hanover* (3), an armed two-masted brig of 120 tons, replaced her predecessor within weeks on the Falmouth to Lisbon route. Following his release from captivity, Captain Sherburn resumed command of the new ship from February 1758.

Hanover (3) sailed from Falmouth on what was to be her last outward voyage on 24 October 1763 carrying a crew of 39. She spent 14 days in Lisbon, during which an armed escort loaded a large iron chest into her stern quarters, containing 20,000 gold moidore (gold coins), then worth about £27,000. She also took on board a heavy and completely illegal private cargo on behalf of the captain, which almost certainly contributed to her loss. This only became known 234 years later after the wreck was re-discovered and excavated. Finally, shortly before she left for Falmouth, her passengers (possibly up to 40 men and women, though accounts of the actual numbers vary) arrived with their baggage and valuables. One of the passengers was reported to be a young man returning to England to take up a large inheritance.

Hanover left Lisbon on 8 November 1763, encountering heavy gales almost immediately. Naturally, these slowed her passage, but no one could have anticipated the easterly hurricane she then met in the English Channel. This was so severe that even with limited reefed sail she was blown clean past Falmouth, totally unable to turn in to the bay. She was then blown past the Lizard still out of control, until she approached Land's End. Conditions on board must have been horrendous, the *Hanover* running before winds of 100 mph, heaving and pitching into gigantic swells. It would have been impossible to prepare any hot food; indeed, the galley would long have extinguished its fire for safety reasons. Even the drinking water cask lashed to the mizzen mast would have become inaccessible, with heavy seas breaking over her decks. As for the passengers and possibly some of the crew, one can imagine their discomfort battened down below decks in cramped airless conditions. We can safely assume that the passengers were in their bunks huddled beneath their blankets or being violently seasick into chamber pots, while those of the crew not on watch would have been in their hammocks, swinging from side to side in the forecastle.

Off Land's End, by steering close inshore the *Hanover* used the relative shelter offered by high cliffs to set what little sail she had left. This enabled her to claw her way round to the

46

north coast of Cornwall past Cape Cornwall until, between Pendeen Point and Gurnard's Head, she found a degree of shelter, conditions eased and the crew prepared to anchor, thinking the worst was over. Whilst Captain Sherburn may not have been familiar with Cornwall's north coast, he would have been aware that there was no suitable port or haven between Land's End and Padstow, many miles further up the coast. The captain was no doubt counting his blessings at having made it to relative safety when, to his horror, the wind changed, veering from east to north-west and increasing in strength, leaving them at its mercy on a lee shore. The storm proved worse than anyone ashore could remember, and now the *Hanover* was between a rock and a hard place, quite literally.

Her captain did his best to save his ship but she was what sailors describe as 'stiff', deep-laden with a heavy cargo, facing an onshore wind and difficult to steer. Somehow she clawed her way past St Ives and St Agnes, but was driven inside of the Bawden Rocks, known generally as 'Man and His Man'. Here, in desperation, she anchored; the crew cut down her masts to reduce windage and threw all her deck cannon overboard to lighten ship, but to no avail. Then during the night she dragged her anchors, going ashore stern first in a rocky gully beneath 300-foot (90-metre) cliffs, where she must have gone to pieces in minutes. No passengers escaped and only three crew, two men and a boy, managed to clamber part way up the cliffs before getting stuck. They were found in a state of exhaustion next morning by tin-miners walking the cliff path to work, who immediately alerted the authorities. The body of Captain

Sherburn was recovered and laid to rest in Falmouth's Parish Church yard, which was fitting since most packet captains had made Little Falmouth or Flushing their home. Other bodies were buried in St Agnes churchyard.

With 'wreckers' lining the cliffs in anticipation of booty, revenue men and Coast Watchers (today called Coastguards) mounted guard on the foreshore to prevent looting and commenced to recover bodies. At the same time, as the tide allowed, they walked out to the wreck probing with iron rods in an attempt to find the bullion chest, but it was already buried by sand and could not be found. However, many of the passengers had taken on board large sums of personal money, which was now lying loose in the shallows. The Collector of Customs for St Ives then enrolled 60 men to search the wreck and came to a verbal agreement with them regarding salvage. One day, when the Collector was in his office in St Ives, he received word that gold coins were being recovered. He hastened back to the wreck, where he found his men scouring the site, one of them holding out his hat into which the others were dropping coins as they were found. The coins were worth 36 shillings each at the time, almost four months' wages to a tin miner, and it is to the credit of these hard-working Cornishmen that the Revenue man later reported that not one coin had been concealed by any of the 60 men.

Over a year later, some time after the insurance for this had already been paid out, the iron chest of bullion was recovered intact from the stern part of the wreck and sent unopened to London, where the cargo of moidores was revealed. With the recovery of what was known to have been the most valuable part of her cargo, the wreck of the *Hanover* was left in peace for the next 229 years.

In 1994 two local salvage divers, Colin Martin and Gerald Cameron, stumbled on the wreck by chance. The story as to why this area was called Hanover Cove was well known, so the divers took a chance and went there in their small boat, to find the wreck completely uncovered and free of sand. Within days they had found and recovered the ship's bell, inscribed in raised letters '*Hanover Paquet 1757*', which removed all doubt that they had found the wreck. They also found a tiny gold mourning ring, missing its original gemstone. The legend engraved on the ring's inner face read '*Mary Sherburn Obit 16 Feb 1748. Age 22*': the late wife of the captain, she had died in childbirth. The ring size is so small it is doubtful it was ever worn by her husband, so it may have been her wedding ring, engraved after her death and worn by Captain Sherburn on a chain around his neck.

With no suitable funding of his own, by 1997 Colin Martin had found enough wealthy investors to mount a full-scale salvage operation, which commenced using an offshore jack-up platform fitted with a crane. This was a unique technique in British wreck salvage at the time, enabling divers to work air-lifts and pressure washing directly on top of the site, the crane ideal to lift artefacts and timbers.

Only then was it discovered that the *Hanover* had been carrying 50 assorted iron cannon as illegal cargo, neatly laid breech to muzzle or top-to-toe in rows in her hold, as well as a large quantity of iron cannon ball ammunition, and boxfuls of flint-lock muskets. So, was Captain Sherburn 'gun-running' on his own account, or had he been ordered by the Packet authorities to bring the cannon to England on their behalf? It's more likely that Sherburn was carrying the cannon illegally, for his own profit, since company rules forbade private cargo, but we will never know for certain.

Before English Heritage closed down the operation with an emergency designation order making the wreck a Protected Site in July 1997, Colin Martin had recovered some 50 cannon and commenced the conservation process by storing them in fresh water. A full-time archaeologist was hired who started work recording the gun sizes, then worked on the pewter and leather artefacts being recovered. In no time at all outside conservation work from other wrecks began to come in, but after the site was designated, financial circumstances dictated the operation be closed down. Twenty of the Finbanker cannon recovered were sold at a Kidderminster auction in 2007 for £1,850 each; but what happened to the remainder is uncertain.

What's left of the *Hanover*?

The site is a Protected Wreck. The National Maritime Museum Cornwall, in Falmouth, holds both the ship's bell and the mourning ring, both of which are on permanent display. A wooden crest recovered at the time of the wreck, which previously was in the old Falmouth Maritime Museum, is also part of the NMMC's collection, along with other small artefacts. Officially it is accepted that the Post Office is the owner of the wreck.

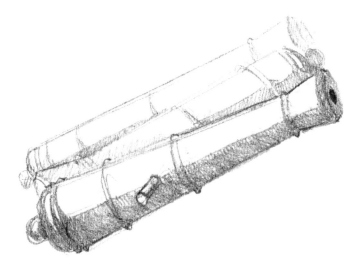

The Finbanker Cannons.

PACKET BRIG *HANOVER*

SIR WILLIAM HAMILTON'S PRICELESS TREASURE
HMS *Colossus*

10 DECEMBER 1798 – SOUTHWARD WELL REEF, SAMSON ISLAND, ISLES OF SCILLY

Life on board HMS *Colossus* in Naples was not easy that autumn in 1798. Now eleven years old and showing her age, she was leaking badly in several places, and was desperately in need of a refit, her crew continually at the pumps. *Colossus* had served under Admiral Sir John Jervis and the recently ennobled Admiral Lord Horatio Nelson for the past two years in the Mediterranean as a store-ship, and was ready to go home. With no permanent naval base in the Mediterranean as yet, she was there to supply stores and spares, hence was constantly on the move in all weathers between Gibraltar, Naples and any ship requiring her services.

Nelson's ship, the 74-gun ship-of-the-line *Vanguard*, badly damaged in the Battle of the Nile at Aboukir Bay and missing an entire mast, had to be towed into the Bay of Naples before she could enter the Royal Dockyard for repairs, using materials supplied by *Colossus*. Nelson had not visited Naples for four years, and his reception was as warm as if he were returning to Portsmouth. Back in 1793, he had made a deep and favourable impression on Sir William Hamilton, the British Minister to the Court of Naples, who introduced him to King Ferdinand and Queen Maria Carolina. Equally charmed by Nelson was Sir William's beautiful but wayward wife, Emma, with whom Nelson later formed an attachment. As the victorious British fleet entered Naples, they were met by a multitude of boats bedecked with flags led by Sir William and Lady Hamilton, followed by the cream of Naples aristocracy. The waiting crowd expected Nelson still to be the man who had bewitched the Court of Naples four years ago but sadly time had taken its toll. Now pale and exhausted, a deep wound showed on his forehead, he had lost the sight of one eye and his right arm had been amputated. Lady Hamilton almost fainted when she saw him, exclaiming 'O God, is it possible?'

Colossus, under the command of Captain George Murray, received her sailing orders on 15 October 1798, which were to convoy the ships ready to sail to the Downs, in Kent. They were to call at Lisbon for water and provisions only, and just sufficient for ten weeks; also *'to receive on board such remittances, in specie, bullion, cochineal, and indigo, as the Merchants of Lisbon may have occasion to make.'*

The *Colossus* already carried in her hold war loot – furniture and guns taken from French ships at the Battle of the Nile. Sir William Hamilton had also added dozens of crates, chests, boxes and parcels of historic 'vases', a mixture of extremely valuable Greek and Etruscan antique pottery. Sir William was an avid art collector and looted countless items from Pompeii and remote tombs in his enthusiasm to create his unique collection. His first collection of antiquities, as he called it, consisting of bronzes, statues, glass ware, coins, gems and jewels, was sold by him to the British Museum for £8,400 (£1 million in 2018). Another of Hamilton's acquisitions was a seven-ton marble vase found in Hadrian's Villa which he offered to the Museum for £350, but unable to afford this sum it went to the Earl of Warwick. So, now ready to sail, at the last minute *Colossus* took on board five more gentlemen passengers, as well as dozens of British and French casualties of the Battle of the Nile, who filled her orlop deck. She also carried the corpse of Admiral Lord Shuldham in a lead coffin, concealed in a plain wooden chest since sailors were superstitious about coffins on board.

Colossus entered St Mary's Roads, the Isles of Scilly, with eight other ships on 7 December 1798, the wind strong from the east and increasing. As her mainsail was furled she slowed, then turned head to wind as her second-best bower anchor was released which took hold in the seabed. Captain Murray ordered a sounding to be taken, which revealed they were in 11 fathoms (66 feet/20 metres). She and her consorts lay quietly at anchor for two days, then on 10 December the wind increased to gale force, and now all 1,700-tons of *Colossus* was reliant on that one anchor and its 8-inch (20-cm) diameter hempen cable, already old and frayed. Only now did Captain Murray regret having given his best anchor to Nelson's *Vanguard*.

As the wind increased, so the top-gallant masts and yards were lowered to reduce windage, but at 4 p.m. her anchor cable parted and she was forced to drop a smaller anchor followed by a sheet anchor. Between them they held the ship secure but for only two hours, since at 6 p.m., having dragged slowly across the sandy seabed the ship took the ground, with only two hours to low water. At midnight her rudder was torn off and four hours later, now full of water, she was resting on the bottom, the sea level with her upper-deck gun ports. Only then were her crew ordered into the rigging. Huge waves swept the length of the ship until the tide fell, allowing the crew to regain the upper deck and swing out her boats. The first men to be landed were the wounded and invalids, and helped by the thirty or so inhabitants of the island of Samson, all the crew were saved bar one, Richard King, a quartermaster, who was washed overboard and drowned whilst taking soundings with a lead and line.

Colossus was lost on Southward Well Reef, and here she slowly broke up lying on her starboard side, her bow towards St Agnes island. Wreckage, barrels, boxes and chests all washed ashore, but only a fraction of Hamilton's collection was salvaged, his priceless treasures left to the mercy of the sea. The Admiralty sent the gun-brig *Fearless* under Lieutenant Pardoe to recover what guns, fittings and stores they could find; even the famous diver John Deane was employed until virtually nothing of value remained, except a few iron cannon, shot and the scattered remains of Hamilton's second collection.

On 8 August 1974, 176 years later, modern divers working for Roland Morris of Penzance re-located the wreck of the *Colossus* and the scattered remains of Sir William Hamilton's once priceless pottery. Over the years countless gales had torn the wreck and the crates of vases to pieces, and now all that remained was the very bottom part of the ship, iron cannon, shot, brass musket and pistol fittings, bottles and thousands of pottery shards. The divers were Mark Horobin, Mike Hicks and 'Slim' McDonald, financed by Morris, who owned the Admiral Benbow Inn in Chapel Street, Penzance. Since 1968 Morris had supported a dive team to work on the 1707 wreck of HMS *Association* after she had been found by Royal Navy divers the previous year. Now Morris hoped that the 'Big-C', as the wreck became known, would yield intact Etruscan pottery, but only one complete item was found, a black spherical Grecian perfume jar which carried the outline of a robed female figure, a truly priceless piece of 2,000-year old history. Otherwise it was countless broken shards, many bearing parts of their original colourful images and decoration. However, the British Museum, which funded the excavation, was able to reassemble a bell krater vase decorated with the painting of the 'Return of Hephaistos' (5th century B.C.).

By coincidence, a few years earlier Richard Larn (the author) and Roland Morris had separately approached John Nott, Member of Parliament for St Ives, requesting him to raise in the House of Commons the matter of recovery of artefact material from historic wrecks in UK waters. In March 1970, under the 'Ten-minute' Rule, Mr Nott proposed an amendment to the Merchant Shipping Act of 1894 to give protection to historic shipwrecks. John Nott's efforts failed but only partially, since in July 1973 a new Protection of Wrecks Act received the Royal Assent.

In May 1975 Morris applied for *Colossus* to be designated a Protected Wreck. *Colossus* was not the first historic shipwreck to receive protection in this way, the *Mary Rose* having received Designation in 1973. Whilst the funding of the recovery of some 35,000 shards was made possible by a British Museum grant of an alleged £40,000, there was a darker side. In their contract with Morris, the Museum had neglected to identify to whom the finds belonged, and when they asked for them to be sent to London, Morris exerted ownership as the salvor and it cost the Museum an almost equal amount to purchase them.

Nature then covered the wreck in metres of sand, but on 4 June 2001 Mac Mace, a well-known commercial diver living on Bryher, found the entire bottom timbers of the *Colossus* had been uncovered by gales. At the same time he found a life-size wooden carving amongst her timbers, a male neo-classical warrior figure now identified as from her port-quarter stern gallery. Designation having expired, Mace re-applied and the site was Designated for the second time in 18 years. At his own expense Mace constructed a custom-made lifting cradle, raised the carving and had it sent to the *Mary Rose* conservation unit at Portsmouth.

The carving is now on public display in Tresco Garden's History Room on the Isles of Scilly. The wreck, which has remained uncovered ever since now has a visiting 'Diver Trail' around it initiated by English Heritage, installed by CISMAS (Cornwall & Isles of Scilly Maritime Archaeological Society).

What remains of the *Colossus* today?

The entire bottom of the ship, holding some 6 to 8 cannon, copper fastening pins in their original position, whole and part muskets, brass fittings from muskets and pistols, iron shot, leather shoes, glass bottles, lead musket shot and rope, survives amongst the timbers. A Diver Trail extends around the wreck site which is a Protected Wreck. For details of the survey work and excavation of the *Colossus*, see the website www.cismas.org.uk/colossus_overview.php. Artefact material is on display in St Mary's Museum, Isles of Scilly, at Charlestown Shipwreck Centre, and in the British Museum, and eBay frequently has small items for sale.

HMS *Colossus*: A part of the design from the shards of Etruscan pottery.

SAIL GIVES
WAY TO STEAM
1807 - 1907

The biggest changes in shipping history took place between 1802 and 1843, as iron slowly replaced the traditional ship-building material of wood, and steam began to challenge the centuries-old use of sail. Experiments in powering boats by steam had been made in France, along the Delaware River in America and in Scotland since the 1780s but the earliest such vessel to demonstrate the practicality of steam power for ships was the paddle-steamer *Charlotte Dundas*, launched in 1803 to tow barges up and down the Forth and Clyde Canal. The first successful passenger-carrying steamboat (named the *Comet* after the Great Comet sighted in 1811) was also built in Scotland and launched in 1812 on the River Clyde.

These early craft plied only inland waterways and estuaries but were followed not long afterwards by the first steam-driven ships to brave the open sea. SS *Savannah*, an American hybrid sailing ship/sidewheel steamer, crossed the Atlantic from Georgia to Liverpool in 1819, but relied mostly on sail power. It was the first steamship to be built of iron, the 116-ton *Aaron Manby*, which holds the distinction not only of making the first direct steam crossing from London to Paris (steaming up the Seine from Le Havre after crossing the English Channel) in 1822 but also the first seagoing voyage by an iron ship anywhere. The era of the transatlantic ocean liner began in the late 1830s with the launch of Brunel's side-wheel paddle steamer SS *Great*

Western. Another British-built steamship, the SS *Archimedes*, which took her maiden voyage from London to Portsmouth in 1839, became the world's first steamship to be driven by a screw propeller instead of paddle wheels. Despite the success of these vessels, most steamships continued to carry masts for auxiliary sails; sailing ships, especially clippers like the *Cutty Sark*, were still being built in large numbers throughout most of the century.

The six shipwreck accounts in this section were predominantly iron or steel vessels, only the Royal Navy frigate HMS *Anson* (pages 58 to 63) and the emigrant barque *John* (pages 64 to 69) being built of wood. It was the rivalry between sail and steam that saw the full-rigged four-masted *Bay of Panama* (pages 76 to 81) built to compete with steam on the Far East trade routes, whilst the gigantic seven-masted schooner *Thomas W. Lawson* (pages 88 to 93) was an American dream with similar ambitions.

Two of the vessels whose stories are told here were huge, steel-built liners, the SS *Schiller* (pages 70 to 75) and the SS *Mohegan* (pages 82 to 87), both carrying wealthy passengers and cargo to and from New York. Both were wrecked respectively on notorious reefs in the Isles of Scilly and south Cornwall. The heavy loss of life in both instances was both tragic and arguably avoidable.

THE WRECK THAT SAVED 10,000 LIVES
FRIGATE HMS *Anson*

29 DECEMBER 1807 – MOUNT'S BAY

Blockade duty in the middle of winter off the coast of France was an unenviable task. None of the crew of the frigate *Anson* were particularly happy with their orders issued by the Admiralty, which were to prevent ships from entering or leaving the Breton port of Brest. It was a task fraught with considerable danger, requiring a continuous patrol up and down the enemy coast with frequent changes of course. The watch on deck was forever attending to her sails and rigging without respite, whilst lookouts in her foretop – their only protective clothing being oilskin coats and sou'wester hats – searched the horizon for any sign of foreign sail. If one should prove to be a French man o'war, then every man aboard would go to his action station and her guns would be manned. If action followed, there would be the hell of cannon fire and the ever-present prospect of death or injury. Uninterrupted sleep between watches was an unheard-of luxury. On top of this, the ship had sailed from Falmouth on Christmas Eve, depriving the married men of the opportunity of being with their families; one of the many unwelcome consequences of England having been more or less continuously at war for nearly 15 years.

The keeper of the Gunwalloe Inn, near Helston, Cornwall, one Henry Cuttance, had happened to be in Falmouth that afternoon and watched the *Anson* leave harbour, towed out past Black Rock by her own ship's rowing boats since there were no tugs at that time. He was feeling rather smug, thanking his lucky stars he was not on board. Taken by the *Anson*'s press gang the day before, he had managed to escape, and derived much pleasure from watching the ship put out to sea. The infamous 'press-gang' was a lawful group of armed officers and sailors from any warship that found itself short of crew. They would patrol the streets, countryside, inns, hostels and brothels, looking for healthy young men they could impress, against their will, literally snatching them off the streets. They would then be taken and put aboard a warship to serve in the Royal Navy for an indeterminate period, often years, with no regard for their circumstances, occupation, wives or family. It was lawful in that only seamen were supposed to be pressed, but in fact it was a brutal and callous form of recruitment regardless of class, age or experience, which did not cease until around 1850.

Under Captain Charles Lydiard, who had commanded *Anson* for two years, she reached her station off Brest, 120 nautical miles due south, a maximum of two days after departure from Falmouth but was unable to remain in the area for long due to a severe WSW gale. The decision to head back for the Lizard, with the intention of returning to Falmouth, was made at the eastern extremity of their patrol, off Roscoff, on 28 December. At 3 p.m. on the 29th, land was seen ahead and the ship's master, Henry Stuart, who was responsible for the ship's navigation whilst the captain was in overall command, calculated they were five miles west of the Lizard, in Mount's Bay, and uncomfortably close in to the shore. They attempted to stand out to sea, but then saw the Lizard up ahead through the fog and realised they were embayed – literally trapped by the wind within the bay with no alternative but to anchor. The best bower was dropped in 20 fathoms (36 metres) with two cables' length of hawser attached and all three top-gallant masts were lowered to deck level to reduce windage. The frigate somehow survived the next 11 hours in mountainous seas with two bow and one midships gun ports completely stove in, causing her to ship tons of water. Then her cable parted, and although her anchor was replaced by the second smaller bower, that cable also snapped leaving the *Anson* adrift. Captain Lydiard was left with little choice: either let the storm drive the ship ashore or attempt to steer her to a place of his choosing. Preservation of life was the priority, so he selected that part of Porthleven's foreshore where two headlands dip down to Loe Pool creating a Bar, one mile east of Porthleven. Unbeknown to the ship's officers, this three-mile stretch of coast is not naturally shelving as one would expect. The shingle beach has a sharp drop-off some 100 metres offshore, creating a steep shelf, which caused the ship to broach to, slewing round leaving her port side parallel to the shore, with her bow facing east.

The *Anson* was built in Plymouth and launched in 1781 as a third-rate, 64-gun ship. During her 26 years of active service, *Anson*'s distinguished record included taking part in the Battle of the Saintes (West Indies) under Admiral Rodney during the American Revolutionary War in 1782, and numerous engagements during the French Revolutionary Wars and Napoleonic Wars since 1793. But during her rebuild in 1794 she was reduced to a 44-gun frigate with her upper deck removed, becoming what was known as a *razée*. As she still carried the same masts, rigging and sails of a much larger ship, she rolled heavily and continually in any sea and was difficult to steer, and had a reputation for being a poor sailer. Now, beam-on to the heavy seas for which Loe Bar is notorious, her mainmast collapsed towards the beach creating a bridge by which survivors could reach the shore. The coast and adjacent cliffs soon became thronged with hundreds of spectators, many of them local miners, news having reached Porthleven and Helston that a large man o'war was in difficulties close inshore and was likely to become a wreck.

The majority of those on board managed to scramble along this floating bridge to safety, despite being frequently part-submerged. There were many men and women[1] too frightened to risk this opportunity to save their lives, who simply gave up and crept away into dark corners of the ship to await their God. The captain, having done all he could to save lives by encouraging them to use the fallen mast, was about to attempt the crossing himself when he heard cries for help from a child. This proved to be a boy of 12 who Lydiard had himself sponsored to join the ship as a captain's servant, eventually to become a midshipman, who lacked the strength and courage to save himself. According to the court-martial following the loss of the ship (quoted by the Curator of Helston Museum, Alderman Frank Strike, in his book *Cornish Shipwrecks*, 1965), Captain Lydiard

'threw one arm around the boy while he cheered him up with words of kind encouragement. With his other arm he clung to the spars and mast, and supported himself and his burden. But the struggle did not last long. Exhausted by the mental and physical sufferings he had endured, he lost his hold not of the boy but of the mast, the waves swept over them and they perished together.'

The number saved from the *Anson* was around 250. Estimates of the number of lives lost vary from 60 to around 190, but an accurate death toll was impossible to establish since many of the men press-ganged in Falmouth only five or six days earlier took the opportunity to desert.

There were many acts of bravery amongst local men and women that day. Several men attempted to swim with ropes out to the wreck but were hurled back ashore by the sea, to be pulled from the breakers badly bruised or with broken limbs, while some even drowned in the attempt. A Mr Roberts of Helston, a powerful swimmer, was the first to reach the ship and clambered aboard; the line he carried was tied to the ship and allowed many to reach the shore in safety. Another local to reach the wreck was Methodist lay preacher William Foxwell of Mullion. He found two women, two children and several crew still alive and helped them overboard to make their way to shore hand over hand on ropes, but unfortunately all the children were lost in the surf.

Amongst the countless spectators was Henry Trengrouse, a 35-year old carpenter and cabinet maker who was born, lived and worked in Helston. He was in his workshop behind 122 Meneage Street, when he heard the news. Curious to see the wreck, he made his way to Porthleven's high cliffs from where he had a grandstand view. A religious man, he was appalled at what he saw: the lifeless corpses floating in the sea, the line of bodies pulled up well above high water mark, and the attempts, sometimes fruitless, of men to reach the wreck. On enquiring what would happen to the bodies, he was informed that a communal grave would be dug on the clifftop in which they would all be buried. Despite heavy rain having set in, Trengrouse stayed watching events until it grew dark before making his way home the three miles to Helston, very unsettled at seeing so many lives lost so close to the shore. His mind was in turmoil: surely there was a method whereby a ship could communicate with the shore

₁ A few women, usually wives of crew members, were generally allowed on board to do the officers' washing, help the ship's cook and, in battle, assist the barber-surgeon treating the wounded. It was thought that their presence helped to improve the atmosphere of the lower deck. The naval expression 'Show a leg' refers to the practice of women dangling a leg outside their hammocks, as they were exempt from the Bosun's call to the sailors to get up in the morning.

or vice versa in similar circumstances?

Arriving home cold, soaked to the skin, exhausted, hungry and depressed, Trengrouse developed a severe chill. His diary recorded:

> *'At the wreck I got very wet from the effects of which and from the cold wind and fatigue, I became much indisposed for several days and was partially confined to my bed. It was then and there that the annihilation of this fine ship and so many of my fellow creatures most seriously arrested my reflections and sympathy, and freshened in my memory the primitive destruction of about fifty fine fellows and soldiers at the wreck of the transport vessel James & Rebecca.'* [2]

After much deliberation the idea of the transfer of a lifeline from ship-to-shore or shore-to-ship seemed to Trengrouse the obvious answer. Inspired by a fireworks display in Helston to commemorate King George III's birthday, he found the solution to his problem. If a thin line could be attached to a rocket and accurately fired from a musket towards the coast or a ship, could not a stronger rope follow, creating a 'bridge' between ship and shore from which a suspended cradle could be hung? The occupant of the cradle could then pull themselves to safety, after which the empty cradle could be pulled back to the ship and used over and over again until all were saved.

In the aftermath of the wreck, on 1 January 1808, Edward Pascoe of Porthleven recovered Captain Lydiard's body from the sea. He was interred at Falmouth with full military honours. Vice Admiral Cotton, the town mayor and the captain's family were at the funeral, and a party of Royal Marines and Militia from Pendennis Castle fired three volleys over the grave. The body was later exhumed and reburied in the family vault in the parish church of Hazelmere, in Surrey. Tobias Roberts and William Foxwell of Helston received silver medals from both the Humane Society and the Navy Board for saving lives, with lesser awards to nine other locals. Strangely, an article printed in the *Cornish Telegraph* almost a hundred years later, in November 1905, credited Trengrouse with having saved lives at the wreck, alleging that he had swum out and saved a child, and that he also dragged to safety a man who would have drowned after being knocked over in the surf. Perhaps there were other unsung heroes that day?

Two important developments came about as the result of the wrecks of the *Anson* and the transport vessel *James & Rebecca*, lost nearby only three weeks earlier. An Act of Parliament (The Burial of Drowned Persons Act), promoted by solicitor Thomas Grylls and Davies Gilbert, MP, both of Helston, was passed on 18 July 1808 which decreed that all bodies cast ashore from the sea were to be laid to rest with Christian rites, in the nearest churchyard at the expense of the Parish. No longer would drowned seamen and passengers be bundled like dead cattle into mass unmarked clifftop graves.

The second development took much longer to be put

[2] This had taken place less than two miles from the *Anson*, only three weeks earlier.

into practice. This was Henry Trengrouse's *Rocket Life Saving Apparatus* which eventually became accepted internationally in 1838, and thereafter was available at every Coastguard Station in Great Britain for 150 years until March 1988, when it was withdrawn in favour of helicopter rescue. At a conservative estimate it saved the lives of at least 10,000 people worldwide. Trengrouse perfected his invention within three months of the wreck of the *Anson*, and cleverly chose a musket to be his rocket's launching platform, knowing that this weapon was in international use both afloat and ashore. Others had similar ideas and Trengrouse's chief rival was Captain George Manby, an army officer who lived in Norfolk. By an incredible coincidence, Manby too had been motivated to invent a 'line-throwing' device having witnessed the destruction of the Royal Navy frigate *HMS Snipe* on the Norfolk coast, near Great Yarmouth in 1807, the same year the *Anson* was lost.

Both men struggled to get either the Government or the Admiralty interested, as both proved parsimonious, and the two inventors spent years getting their apparatus accepted. Manby's Mortar Apparatus eventually received recognition by a Parliamentary Committee in 1809, and he was awarded £2,000 (the equivalent of some £200,000 today), but despite recommendations that the apparatus be employed across the country it was installed at only a few coastal locations. Trengrouse's invention eventually won the day for which he received the recognition he fully deserved; using powerful pyrotechnics developed and supplied by John Dennett, the Rocket Life Saving Apparatus went into use worldwide after 1838.

Captain Manby died in poverty in a basement flat in Great Yarmouth in 1854 aged 89, destitute, bitter, unrecognised and forgotten. In another coincidence, Henry Trengrouse died the same year, aged 82, surrounded by his family in his house at 122 Meneage Street, Helston, which today carries a commemorative blue plaque recognising his achievement. It is quite remarkable that these two men, living at opposite ends of the country, who had both pursued the same goal after witnessing different tragic shipwrecks in 1807 which completely changed their lives, died in the same year without ever having met each other.

What remains of the *Anson* today?

Four of the *Anson*'s huge iron cannon, each mounted on replica gun carriages, survive, the author being part of the diving team responsible. One is on the quay at Porthleven, another outside the Helston Folk Museum and the other two are inside the entrance to HMS *Seahawk*, the Royal Naval Air Station at Culdrose, on the Lizard peninsula. Within the Helston Museum can be seen two of Trengrouse's wooden chests that held his apparatus, the contents displayed on wall boards or in cabinets. The wreck itself lies some 100 metres (328 feet) offshore from the very centre of Loe Bar at Porthleven in a depth of 10 to 15 metres (22 to 49 feet). Several iron cannon remain embedded in the decayed or concreted layer holding the remains of iron fittings and cannon balls, but no timber survives. The wreck site has no special protected status.

189 EMIGRANT PASSENGERS DROWNED
BARQUE *John*

3 MAY 1855 – MANACLE ROCKS, THE LIZARD

In 1803 the sheer number of migrants from Great Britain and Ireland to America and Canada caused Parliament to enact legislation to regulate vessels carrying emigrants. Canada in particular was crying out for mechanics and labourers, and offered 'assisted passage' in steerage to those who could not afford to pay, whilst those travelling cabin class paid £2 each, but supplied their own provisions. In 1850, eighty vessels arrived in Quebec with 9,135 passengers, after Atlantic crossings of between 27 and 39 days. Those from England received the sum of 20 shillings on landing and, having passed through quarantine, were usually met by organisations who arranged employment within a few days, mostly in railroad construction or domestic service.

The three-masted barque *John*, of 468 tons, registered in Plymouth, built in 1810 at Chester, had undergone a refit at Cardiff in 1855. Her owners, Messrs Rawle & Co, Merchants, had spent £200 on the work, but it was later established that she carried only four lifeboats, insufficient for the number on board, and that she had no signal guns or distress rockets. Her classification at Lloyd's had long expired and had not been renewed, despite the refit. This may also have been her first emigrant voyage since, although the mate stated at the inquiry that he had been on two previous voyages with the captain to Quebec, records of emigrant ships sailing from Plymouth make no reference to the *John*.

In Plymouth a Government Emigration Depot was created in 1847, administered by the Colonial Land and Emigration Commissioners. This was located at the site of the old naval Victualling Yard at Lambhay, Plymouth, which had storehouses at Elphinstone Wharf, between Phoenix Wharf and Fisher's Nose, capable of accommodating 500 people. Here poor emigrants would gather to have their Emigration Orders checked and where they would also receive a rudimentary health check and basic board and lodgings until their ship sailed. The Emigration Agent at the Depot in 1855 was Lieutenant Carew RN, and he supervised the whole process, from arrival to departure. He was required to maintain meticulous lists and ledgers, but it was the responsibility of the ship's master to prepare his passenger list and deposit it at the Plymouth Custom House before sailing.

The *John*, under 34-year old Captain Edward Rawle, who was also the major share-holder of the several owners of the same surname, carried a crew of 19 (the number would have been 20 but an apprentice, William Hughes, who was scheduled to join the ship, failed to sign on). As to the number of passengers she carried, every printed account of the disaster varies, from 210 to 350, of which 120 were children. The Bodmin Court proceedings of 2 August 1855, when Captain Rawle was tried on a charge of manslaughter, stated that there were 260 steerage passengers, a figure which should be accepted as accurate.

Where had these emigrants come from? Literally across the West Country: from St Ives, Stithians and Bodmin in the west, to Newton Abbot, Plymouth and Dartmoor in Devon, and even two from the Channel Isles. Once checked in, each family was allocated a room with wooden bunks in the Emigration Depot, staying there (apart from meal times) until the ship was ready. They were then herded down to the dock, up the ship's gangway and down into the gloomy, damp, steerage deck where each family stacked their belongings, and claimed bunk spaces. The five cabin passengers quartered in the deck house were described at the Court of Inquiry as being 'of superior character'.

The *John* sailed out of Plymouth Sound at 4 p.m. on the afternoon of 3 May 1855 with both the captain and mate William Goodwin on deck, Able Seaman Andrew Elder at the wheel, steering a westerly course as ordered. The wind was NNW, conditions fair, the sea calm, and as it grew dusk an almost full moon meant it was spring tides. At 7 p.m. A.B. Elder was relieved at the helm by A.B. William Rowe who received instructions from the captain to maintain the same course. Rowe did not remain at the helm for long when he was relieved by an A.B. Bennett, who in turn was relieved by A.B. Edward Venning and then A.B. James Curry. It is quite remarkable that by the time the *John* struck the Manacles, six hours after sailing and still only 40 miles from Plymouth, there had been five different seamen at the helm.

The mate stayed on deck until 8.30 p.m., leaving Elder still at the wheel steering WSW, the captain on the poop, by which time they had passed Dodman Point, an estimated four miles off to starboard. The mate went down to his cabin under the poop deck, where he partially undressed and got into his hammock, but was woken at about 10 p.m. when the ship struck rocks. He went out on deck, joining the large number of passengers who were just standing around. He then went down into the hold where he found 5 feet (1.5 metres) of water. Returning to the poop to report his findings to the captain, he ran to the now unmanned wheel only to find that the ship's rudder was gone. He shouted to the captain it was impossible to steer, then gave orders for the seamen to trim the yards and let her run ashore. The *John* ran in a further 400 yards (528 metres), then went hard aground, between Dean Point and Chynhalls Point (possibly in what some called Godrevy Cove), within 200 feet (61 metres) of the coast. Now lashed by heavy seas, the captain ordered the port anchor to be dropped, to prevent the ship drifting any further inshore as the tide rose.

By now, despite being half tide, there was some 18 inches (45 cms) of water over the upper deck, leaving the poop deck only 5 feet (1.5 metres) clear of the sea. Captain Rawle then gave orders to lower the boats, the quarter boat first, which being small could only hold 14 people at the most. A.B. Curry, who was manning the lowering tackle, then got into the boat along with the captain, but as it got close to the sea the captain climbed back on deck. There was speculation in the press prior to the inquiry that the captain had in fact deserted his ship, remaining in the quarter boat, but that was not true. No sooner had four male passengers (one of whom had the surname Solomon) boarded the boat, than the rope painter parted and the boat drifted away in the dark. Finding there were oars in the boat but no thole pins or rowlocks, A.B. Curry got the men to hold up a bottom grating to act as a sail whilst he steered with an oar until they landed safely at Coverack.

The crew then attempted to get the main lifeboat into the water, but while lifting it over the ship's rail several planks were stove in, rendering it useless. Turning their attention to the long-boat, which was capable of holding 35 persons, the captain ordered the crew to wait until daylight, so it was left hanging on the davits just clear of its chocks, which proved a mistake. An hour later as the tide rose, a heavy swell swept the long-boat away, leaving only a pinnace with a capacity of 16 to 20 people. By now all the passengers were on deck attempting to get above the waves, dozens

on the poop along with most of the children. A few were clinging to the main and mizzen mast shrouds, despite the captain and mate pleading with them to get as high in the rigging as they could. Disaster struck when the ropes holding the main boom parted and, in swinging round, catapulted dozens of men, women and children into the sea. There were countless terrifying scenes that night, as the tide rose and more and more passengers were washed overboard, whilst above the roar of the sea and the sounds of the ship breaking up could be heard the screams and sobbing of women and children. Captain Rawle did all he could to assist, offering comfort, holding children, keeping them safe whilst the parents got into the rigging before passing them up. He eventually went up into the maintop himself to save his own life, taking a child with him.

By 5.30 a.m. as it was just beginning to get light, there was 12 feet (3.5 metres) of water over the upper deck and waves were still sweeping passengers overboard. At 6 a.m. the Coverack Coastguards saw the wreck from their look-out, with some 60 to 70 people still clinging to the rigging. Thomas Clear, senior coastguard, told the subsequent inquiry that they proceeded to Porthoustock where they found that the local men knew nothing of the incident. By noon they had three boats ready to launch, but one was over-manned and was forced back to shore. The sea was now running so heavily on the shoreline that it was 1.30 p.m. before a boat, manned by Thomas Clear, Mark Townsend, Daniel Baker, John George and John Matthews, could be launched. They made three trips to the wreck, saving 35 in total. In the meantime an improvised raft, put together on board, was found holding nine men and one woman, all of whom were saved by the Porthoustock boat. A second boat, manned by James Hill, William Matthews, Thomas Pearce, Henry Tripconey and James Connor, saved 50, landing them at Tom's Cove where locals hauled them up the cliff face using ropes. A total of 189 passengers were lost, yet every single one of the crew, including Captain Rawle, survived, some of them stepping into the boat in which they were rescued carrying their belongings in bags! Perhaps the most heartrending scene for survivors and locals alike was the eventual line of many dead children, lying side by side on Porthoustock beach, awaiting identification.

On Saturday 5 May, less than two days after the disaster, the District Coroner, John Carlyon of Truro, opened an inquest with a jury in the Red Lion inn, St Keverne, to which various members of the crew and passengers, together with coastguards from Coverack and Porthoustock, were called to testify. By the end of the three-day inquest, the *John's* captain, Edward Rawle, was formally charged with the manslaughter of Eliza Hallett, a token female victim of the wreck, and he was taken to Bodmin to await trial. Later a separate charge was brought against two local people, accused of looting the dead bodies. Fifty-one survivors from the wreck were conveyed back to Plymouth by the steamship *Avon* on 8 May, but for those who had drowned, a mass grave was dug in St Keverne's churchyard and 123 bodies were laid to rest, at a charge to the parish of £155.7s.1d.

At the trial of Captain Rawle, which opened at the Cornwall Assizes in Bodmin on 2 August 1855, every aspect of the shipwreck was investigated. Captain William Lory, RN, who had commanded Post Office Packets out of Falmouth for nine years, was the expert witness on maritime matters and ship handling. He had regularly taken Packet vessels to Plymouth for refit, so knew the south coast of Cornwall well. He criticised Captain Rawle for taking a course of WSW from Rame Head, which he explained would take the ship directly onto the Manacles, whereas had the course been SW by W, which was only one point further south, this would have seen the *John* pass the Lizard four or five miles off to the south. The conduct of Captain Rawle following the stranding of the ship was also questioned, passengers on board stating they had implored the captain to launch the boats but that he had said they should wait till morning.

One of the three counsels for the prosecution, Serjeant Kinglake, attorney-at-law addressed the hearing saying:

'Captain Rawle appeared to show want of skill and judgement prior to the disaster in not properly piloting the ship, and after the ship struck he again betrayed a want of skill and ability in providing for the safety of the crew and passengers....The women and children were on the poop of the vessel, and the crew in the rigging, the captain with them, while the ship lay at the mercy of the waves. I shall prove to you that the women and children were swept away from the poop sometimes a dozen at a time, and so this melancholy state of things continued till the morning when boats from the shore came to the wreck and received those who were living.

To show you the serious importance of this case I will tell you that 190 poor souls met their death on this occasion, who were chiefly those who crowded the poop. There were not I believe any men there.'

As the trial drew to a close, the owners of the *John* advised the court they had already placed £3,500 into the hands of the Board of Trade as security arising out of the loss of the vessel (£320,000 by current values). Mr Justice Williams then summed up the trial, and at 7 p.m. asked the jury to retire to consider their verdict. They returned after only five minutes' deliberation, returning a verdict of 'Not Guilty'. Officers of the court were then said to have

'quelled the signs of approbation that resulted from the jury's decision'.

Another trial which took place at Bodmin at the same time was of Matilda Gay, aged 35, and Constantine Tripconey, 62, a St Keverne shoemaker, who were charged jointly with stealing on or about 31 May ten sovereigns from a dead body at St Keverne. The unidentified corpse was a woman found on Porthoustock beach. The defendants had reportedly found a sewn-up pocket in the woman's stays, cut it open and removed the gold coins. The jury thought they had not taken the money with the intention of committing a felony, whereupon the judge, 'with evident astonishment', said 'did they take the money with felonious intent?' The jurymen were, according to the court proceedings,

'as stupid a body of men as could well be got together, and it was some time before they could understand the judge.'

Eventually both Gay and Tripconey were found guilty and sentenced to three months' imprisonment, the female to hard labour.

What remains of the *John* today?

To date, as far as we know, the remains of the wreck have never been found or positively identified. The ship would certainly have had a bell, which is likely to have carried a name, but its current whereabouts is not known. One might expect that such a disaster would warrant some sort of prominent epitaph, but this is not the case: those who died in this unprecedented disaster are remembered today by an upright slate headstone in St Keverne churchyard which reads:

'SACRED TO THE MEMORY OF 120 PERSONS
HERE INTERRED
WHO WERE DROWNED IN THE WRECK OF THE
JOHN, MAY 3, 1855'

CORNWALL'S *TITANIC* LINER SS *Schiller*

SS *Schiller* was a 3,421-ton German ocean liner, one of the largest vessels of her time. Launched in 1873, she plied her trade across the Atlantic Ocean, carrying passengers between New York and Hamburg for the German Transatlantic Steam Navigation Line. Having left America ten days earlier, on 7 May 1875 the *Schiller* was approaching the Bishop Rock west of the Isles of Scilly, en route to Hamburg via Plymouth and Cherbourg, when the ship became blanketed in dense fog. First Mate Heinrich Hillers, on the bridge, who had a Master's ticket in sail, had experienced thick weather countless times but admitted to his captain that he had never seen it as thick as this at sea. Suggesting they change course, he said

'It would be prudent and far safer to spend the night further out in the English Channel and wait for the fog to clear, than continue blindly at full speed'.

But Captain Johannes Georg Thomas had other priorities: such as arriving in Plymouth on schedule to land passengers. He felt sure they were still some 20 to 25 miles offshore, but nevertheless rang the engine-room telegraph to reduce to half-speed, so that she was now making only 6 knots. Like many early steamships, the *Schiller* still carried sails on both masts as an economy measure, and Chief Boatswain Simon Jensen and his watch were aloft furling them when the captain reduced speed even further to dead-slow.

The time was 10 p.m., and most of her 195 steerage and first-class cabin passengers were either in their bunks or on deck, hoping to see the islands and their first glimpse of England. The more affluent socialite first-class passengers, all 59 of them, were mostly in the saloon, talking, drinking or playing cards, whilst in the background a piano was being played. Most of those who anticipated leaving the ship at Plymouth the next morning had retired early, including Susan Duckfield and Frances Evans and their five children, whilst Joseph Legenore from Kentucky was due to disembark at Cherbourg later in the day, so he had already taken to his bunk at 9 p.m. These passengers survived and later made statements about their movements to the subsequent inquiry.

It may not be unique, but there can't be many instances when a ship's captain asks his passengers to volunteer as lookouts, offering as a reward a bottle of champagne to the first man to see the Bishop Rock lighthouse or hear its fog bell! It is interesting to note that Captain Thomas said the 'first man', rather than the 'first man or woman', suggesting he did not think women would make good lookouts, but it was irrelevant since the prize was never claimed anyway.

One hour later a deep rumbling noise was followed by a shuddering sensation as the *Schiller* ran over rocks, then struck a larger obstruction with her port side and came to a complete stop. The captain gave the order to go full astern, which successfully pulled the ship part way clear of the rocks only to be thrown back by heavy seas, beam-on. On the bridge, the captain called out 'Are we in collision with another ship?', then rang down to stop the engine. Instead of being some seven miles west of the Isles of Scilly and the Bishop Rock lighthouse, they were close inshore of the light and amongst the infamous Western Rocks.

Orders were immediately given for soundings to be taken of the *Schiller*'s bilges to see if her hull had been penetrated. The ship's siren was continuously sounded, but tragically this distress call was ignored as it was the custom in the Scillies for a ship to indicate her safe passage by firing a minute gun. The lifeboats were uncovered and prepared for lowering. With all the ship's officers on deck, the Purser reported that the forward part of the ship was rapidly filling as the sea poured in. Passengers were now streaming up from below, many of them still in flimsy night attire and totally bewildered by the impenetrable fog and the noise of the siren. When word spread that the ship was on the rocks and already filling with water, consternation was followed by panic.

Second Mate Erwin Polemann was about to tell the captain that Chief Engineer Leonard Fahrig had said the engine-room was still dry, when a fireman interrupted to say the boiler room was filling with water and about to extinguish the fires. At that moment the entire ship lurched as her bottom hull plates ruptured, and with her bow trapped she swung round with the tide and took a heavy list to starboard. The *Schiller* was now in an impossible situation and beyond being saved. Aground and filling rapidly at dead of night in dense fog, with a heavy sea running, her upper deck covered in panic-stricken passengers and crew, the situation was grim. Captain Thomas attempted to regain control by firing his pistol, but the noise of the wind, the crashing waves on the rocks, steam pressure being released from her boilers and the screaming of passengers completely drowned out his orders and chaos ensued.

Life jackets were issued, and all eight boats ordered to be readied for launching. For her time, *Schiller* was well-equipped: six boats were double-ended 28-foot long lifeboats, stowed abreast of her two funnels, the other two being gigs stowed on the quarter deck aft. Between them they had a potential capacity to hold 400 people, but hysteria gripped many of the passengers and men were clambering into lifeboats whilst the crew were still trying to prepare them, making them impossibly heavy to swing out and lower into the sea. Fighting then broke out, not helped by the ship's firemen, who had gathered all the spirits they could find in the saloon and got hopelessly drunk. Meanwhile, of those boats lowered all but two either filled with water or capsized, two being crushed when a funnel collapsed across them. Then just before midnight the fog thinned, then cleared, and the beam of the Bishop Rock lighthouse, only two-thirds of a mile away, swept over the wreck. The two lifeboats which got away were only part-full, drifting off into the night eventually to land on Tresco with just 26 men and one woman, leaving 320 still aboard.

The captain then ordered all the 50 women and children left on aboard to get into the deckhouse above the waves, but shortly afterwards a huge sea ripped off the deckhouse roof and sucked its occupants overboard, never to be seen again. The two gigs successfully launched but had a harrowing time before they reached land. Gig No. 7, with survivors who had been rescued from lifeboat No. 5, attempted to reach St Agnes, but when the fog returned they lost their way. After rowing and drifting for over eight hours they eventually entered Tresco Channel and landed at New Grimsby. The other gig, No. 8, had no compass and had been rowed for an hour when they heard voices and rescued two passengers, Charles Frahm and Charles Percy, the latter barely conscious, from the sea. There were now ten people on board, and after ten hours' rowing they found themselves at Gimbal Porth, Old Grimsby, on the other side of Tresco!

At dawn, the first on the scene was a Sennen Cove fishing boat which saved seven men, two of whom died from exposure, then a flotilla of local boats arrived as well as the *Lady of the Isles* steam packet. It has been impossible to establish an exact figure of the numbers of passengers and crew aboard the liner, as contemporary records vary so much. However, it is known that only 43 survived (15 passengers, including one woman, and 28 crew), which means that at least 312 and probably many more lost their lives, the largest number of victims of any one shipwreck in Cornwall and the islands, apart from the HMS *Association* disaster of 1707 (see pages 32 to 37). A full account of this terrible tragedy, including the inquiry which followed it, may be found in *The Victorian Titanic*: *The Loss of the SS Schiller in 1875*, by Keith Austin (Halsgrove, 2001).

Dealing with the aftermath of such a tragic shipwreck as the *Schiller* was no easy task. Bags of mail and bodies were turning up all over the islands, each corpse having to be searched for identification and possessions, which would be recorded before burial. One example was:

'Warrant No.3. 08.05.1875. Dead body of male, ship's doctor – Anton G. Sanders. Had three coats on, outside contained pocket book which held the passport of George Lenkland, Citizen of New York. 17 dollars, 65 cents found on inside clothing, plus 90 large gold coins; 23 small gold coins; 2 large silver coins; 2 rings; 2 brooches; 1 crucifix; 3 lockets; 10 ear-drops; 5 pins; 18 studs; 1 pencil case; 1 silver whistle; 1 pair of bracelets; sundry small coins; 2 watches and 3 chains. Body picked up near the site of the wreck by T. Beeston, delivered to the Quay by William Pender and crew of the St. Agnes gig, Gem.'

Thirty-seven interments took place in Old Town churchyard a week after the wreck, followed by 110 seven days later. These included 66 adult males, 34 adult females, five boys and two girls. Four males were buried on St Agnes and one on St Martin's. With no real depth of soil anywhere on St Mary's, the digging of three mass graves was a problem and explosives had to be used to remove the rocks. Several victims were later exhumed, embalmed and sent back to New York for family burials in America, the bodies fortunately identified by their name on the coffin and a wooden marker above ground. The German Government reimbursed the islands for the cost of the burials and shipment of coffins to other countries.

Amongst the dead was a Dr Susan Dimock who, though only 28 years old, was a pioneer in American medicine, as the first woman member of the North Carolina Medical Society who had become resident physician of the New England Hospital for Women and Children only three years earlier. She was buried in one of the mass graves, then exhumed by request and her body returned to her home city, after being embalmed by a Dr Hoggan from the medical college in Boston, who was in London at the time and travelled to Scilly specially to carry this out.

The ship's manifest shows that she carried 2,000 tons of valuable cargo, including 250 bags of mail, tobacco, clocks, 67 harvest reapers, honey, corn, sewing machines, cotton etc and $300,000, equivalent to £60,000 in sterling, in $20 gold coins (15,000 coins in total) in six wooden kegs. Salvage of the gold specie proved difficult since the kegs had been smashed open in the wreck, making it hard for divers to locate the coins. Eventually the equivalent of £57,712 was recovered, and of the £2,288 left behind a considerable number of coins have since been found by modern divers.

What remains of the *Schiller* today?

The wreck lies scattered along the northern side of Retarrier Ledges. She was heavily salvaged by the Western Marine Salvage Company of Penzance in the 1920s; therefore, little is identifiable other than the iron propeller and shaft at the stern, and the anchors and chain near the bow.

The ship's bell, damaged but bearing her name and the date 1873, is in private hands on St Mary's, as are other artefacts including saloon cutlery and dishes, serviette rings, a champagne cooler, a silver tray and silver teapots (all bearing the crest of the German Transatlantic Steam Navigation Co.), and some of the $20 gold coins. Also salvaged was a set of silver cutlery marked 'L.B', a wedding present to Louise Becker (aged 50 at the time of her death), who had lived at West 56th Street, New York. The St Mary's Museum displays a number of artefacts and photographs, and the largest reminder is the memorial obelisk at the highest point of Old Town churchyard, inscribed:

'In Memory of Louise Holzmeister, born at New York, 15 May 1851, who lost her life in the wreck of the SS Schiller on the Scilly Isles, 7 May 1875. Her body rests in the deep, this monument has been erected to her memory as a mark of affection by a sorrowing husband.'

A mail bag from SS *Schiller.*

FROZEN TO DEATH IN THE RIGGING
FULL-RIGGED SHIP *Bay of Panama*

10 MARCH 1891 – NARE POINT, OFF PORTHALLOW

This four-masted steel ship, which started life in 1883 as Yard No.164 in the shipyard of Harland & Wolff, Belfast, was the last to be built of five similar ships. Coming after sail had been largely ousted from the Australian wool and emigrant trade in favour of steamships, this class of ship were generally called 'clippers' and had enormous capacity, capable of carrying huge quantities of coal, nitrate, wool, jute or tea. The *Bay of Panama* was one such carrier and, at 2,365-tons gross, she was huge. From the end of her spike-bowsprit to the upper strake of her whaleback poop, she measured 340 feet (103.6 metres), 130 feet longer than the immortal *Cutty Sark*. Her mainmast from deck level to the truck at the top of the mast towered 140 feet (42.6 metres), almost the height of Nelson's Column in Trafalgar Square. Her yards carried a total of eight acres of best quality Baltic flax sail.

Unfortunately, all five of the sailing ships built on this model had chequered and mostly short lives. The *Bay of Biscay* (built like the *Bay of Panama* for J. and G. Bullock & Co. of London, but at Govan on the Clyde) disappeared in a South Atlantic gale in 1880 and the *Bay of Cadiz*, built in 1878, sank in the Pacific in 1889. The *Bay of Naples* (built at Aberdeen, also for J. and G. Bullock & Co.) suffered near capsizing and a serious fire and, after being sold to Russia in 1897, one of her boats capsized in New Caledonia and 14 of her crew were eaten by sharks. The *Star of Bengal*, built by Harland & Wolff in 1874, lasted longer but in 1908, three years after her purchase by the Alaska Packers' Association, she was wrecked off Coronation Island with few survivors, remaining in the top five maritime disasters in Alaskan history. However, the most macabre fate was reserved for the *Bay of Panama*, the largest of this ill-fated quintet.

The *Bay of Panama* had spent her life trading in Calcutta jute between India and Great Britain. In October 1890 the vessel received instructions from her owners, J. and G. Bullock & Co. of London, to proceed up the Hooghly River to Calcutta and take on board 3,000 tons of jute from Ralli Brothers, a highly successful Greek expatriate business with offices in Calcutta. 13,000 bales duly arrived by rail on flat-bed trucks and were then ferried out by barge to the ship lying at anchor mid-stream. The individual bales, each weighing about 336 lbs (152 kgs), were jammed in tight layers throughout the ship's holds. Wooden hatch covers were then fitted, covered overall with three layers of heavy canvas held in place by flat iron bars sitting in angle brackets, secured by wooden wedges. The *Bay of Panama* left Calcutta on 18 November 1890 under tow of a paddle-tug, with 36 crew and one passenger, Captain David Wright's wife. The crew were Chief Officer Bullock of Birmingham; second officer Allnut of Hull; four apprentices, Beresford, Forbes, Allport and Ingliss; an Irish carpenter; a Scottish sailmaker; an American bosun; a Welsh bosun's mate; four quartermasters; a cook; a steward and 19 seamen.

The *Bay of Panama's* passage from Calcutta to Dundee, via the Cape of Good Hope, was estimated at 120 days, and she sighted the Lizard lighthouse in the English Channel on Sunday 8 March, only a week behind schedule. She was still under full sail, heading ESE on the port tack when the wind commenced to freshen, causing the captain to shorten sail.

By 1861 the government's Meteorological Office was issuing printed weather forecasts in ports, but with no wireless telegraphy on many ships until well after the turn of the century, weather warnings could not be communicated to mariners once ships were at sea, leaving their captains to rely on 'weather-lore' acquired in their seafaring career. Around the UK coastline from 1862, coastguard stations displayed storm warning cones when appropriate, which were helpful to coastal sea traffic but of no use to vessels off-shore which would be out of sight. Had the *Bay of Panama*

been aware of the impending hurricane in her path, she could well have taken avoiding action, possibly by riding out the storm mid Channel and probably surviving, but it was not to be.

During the afternoon watch the Lizard lighthouse was seen again off her port-quarter, the wind continuing to increase so that sail was further reduced to lower topsails and the crew were ordered to batten down for an impending storm. Later that afternoon the wind increased to hurricane force. The rising sea caused the ship to roll heavily and with waves now breaking across her deck, the crew were unable to go aloft in such conditions. At 8.30 p.m. the sails on both the fore and spanker masts were blown to shreds. All that night the *Bay of Panama* lay hove-to under bare poles at the mercy of the wind and tide, with not a scrap of canvas set on her four masts. They were in fact caught in the centre of what later became known as the 'Great Blizzard' of 1891, a storm more severe than any within living memory.

At 7 a.m. on Monday 9 March, the captain ordered the bosun's mate Frederick Evans to take a sounding, which revealed a depth of 50 fathoms (300 feet/91 metres) with white sand in the tallow. They were in deep water, and safe: or so Captain Wright thought. All that day the hurricane continued with tremendous seas and by midnight was accompanied by heavy snow. This was so intense that the lookouts left the forecastle to report to Captain Wright that they could not keep their eyes open due to the heavy driving flakes. Sleep was impossible and the crew, except for the captain and the deck watch on the poop deck, were in their bunks, wide-awake, braced against being thrown to the deck. They literally had no idea where the ship was, other than that they were somewhere between the Lizard and Falmouth.

In preparing for the storm they had taken every seamanlike precaution, but these conditions were way beyond anything the crew had experienced before. In the forecastle where most of the crew lived, the midships deckhouse and officers' poop deck cabins, kitbags, suitcases, clothing, china, food, bottles, books and personal belongings were thrown from their stowage to litter the accommodation decks. Meanwhile, all the ship's boats had been smashed to pieces and deck fixtures and fittings were either bent out of shape or torn from their mountings. The maelstrom could only be described as 'an overpowering influence for destruction' (as it was reported in the *West Briton* newspaper). Yet it is interesting that The Times newspaper's weather forecast for that day (9 March) had said 'moderate NE winds, generally fair'!

At 1.30 a.m. on 10 March there was a sudden ominous screeching sound as the *Bay of Panama*'s hull plating scraped over rock. The ship shuddered as she drove ashore, bow first, onto the rocks a little south of Nare Point, only a few hundred yards from Porthallow beach. The hurricane immediately pushed the ship round till her port side was parallel to the coast, her starboard side beam-on to mountainous seas. In the Falmouth Receiver of Wrecks' Deposition Book (1888–1907), Able Seaman Andreas Gabrielsen recorded that the captain and mate, who had

been on the forecastle, had gone aft and fired a distress rocket *before* the ship struck. However, the bosun's mate Evans, the eventual senior surviving crew member, swore that the rocket was fired sometime *after* she struck, which makes more sense. In any event, due to the driving snow, no one saw the flares from the land and soon afterwards a huge wave swept away not only the second mate, but also swamped the main cabin, washing the captain, his wife and six members of the crew over the side.

It was not until dawn that a local farmer, William Nicholls of Penare Farm, saw the wreck whilst out searching for his sheep in the snow, now over 6 feet deep in places. He struggled back to the fishing village of Porthallow, where he informed the coastguard, William Ashley. In turn the coastguard summoned the Coverack Rocket Life-Saving Apparatus horse-drawn wagon, which with some difficulty reached the high cliffs overlooking the wreck scene by 9 o'clock in the morning.

A grisly sight met the eyes of the rescuers. The *Bay of Panama* was now a total wreck; her mizzenmast had collapsed and both fore and main topmasts had broken off and fallen into the sea along with their yards and sail. Rigging, ropes and tattered canvas lay strewn the length of her port side in a complete jumble, hanging down into the sea. After the captain was swept overboard, the mate had taken charge and ordered the remaining crew to take to the rigging to get above the raging sea but the freezing spray which showered the rigging turned quickly to ice and at least six rigid bodies, some frozen to death, all sheathed in ice, were found clinging to the heavy steel shrouds supporting the ship's lower fore and mainmasts. During the long wait before dawn the bosun, who had also been swept into the water but managed to clamber back aboard and sought shelter in the mizzen rigging, had gone out of his mind and deliberately jumped into the freezing water. Eighteen survivors, some of whom had had to be lifted from the rigging with their limbs in the position in which they had been found, being incapable of movement, were taken off the forecastle by breeches buoy and the last of these, Ordinary Seaman Wilfred Drysdale, told Chief Coastguard Officer Gibson that only the dead remained aboard.

There followed two acts of bravery that deserve special mention. Several of the rescuers insisted that at least one man on the poop deck was still alive, saying they had seen limb movement. Volunteers were called for and both Coastguard James Lewis and Coastguard Boatman William Pond-Fisher were hauled off to the wreck by breeches buoy. At the break of the poop they met the ghastly sight of the two quartermasters, Sanders and Costain, frozen solid in the lower rigging, swinging to and fro as the ship rolled. Below them another man lay face down and rigid on deck, whilst Apprentice Ingliss was down on one knee, one arm hooked over the rail, eyes wide open staring sightless into the blizzard. The two rescuers were then hauled back ashore, utterly traumatised by the experience, icicles already forming on their hats. The lines to the ship were then cut but convinced that men were still alive on board, another volunteer was called for to swim out to the wreck

and James Cliff stepped forward. Despite this rescue bid going no further, Cliff's willingness and bravery and that of Lewis and Pond-Fisher was indisputable.

The survivors were taken to Penare Farm, near St Keverne, thawed out, fed and put to bed. Next day they trudged the two miles through snow drifts to St Keverne where a local horse-drawn carrier's bus got them as far as Gweek but deep drifts prevented any further progress in their journey to Falmouth. Four hours later, a pathetic procession of 18 survivors, many of them with bare feet, found its way to Falmouth's High Street and the Royal Cornwall Sailors' Home. As the *Falmouth Packet* newspaper reported,

'They endured as much privation in that walk as they did in the actual shipwreck.'

And so only half of those who had embarked on the *Bay of Panama* eventually returned to their homes and families.

Two days later, the storm having abated, the steamer Hermes, owned by the Neptune Salvage Company of Cowes, Isle of Wight, entered Porthallow Bay to inspect the wreck. The salvage work was carried out by two Liverpool divers, who set up a boiler and steam donkey-engine on the deck of the *Bay of Panama* to operate a winch. By using one of the ship's yards as a crane boom, they commenced to recover the burlap-encased bales of jute, which were transhipped into barges alongside. No actual diving was required until the top layers were taken out, then the men took turns to enter the hold and put strops around the sodden bales until the entire cargo was salvaged and later forwarded to Dundee. After washing to remove the salt water, this vegetable matter known as the 'golden fibre', second only to cotton in the amount grown, was made into burlap, hessian, gunny cloth, twine, rope, matting, coffee sacks, sandbags, wall covering and furnishings.

The salvage work was interrupted that August when the donkey boiler burst, killing one of the divers and sending pieces of metal as high as the clifftop. Sightseers came in their hundreds to see the wreck and hear tales of the crew's ordeal. Timber from her decks was cut into small pieces and sold as souvenirs, and the ship's bell donated to a small Helford Passage church where it still hangs in a pointed tower, weather-beaten and green with verdigris.

During the period of 9 to 13 March 1891 the 'Great Blizzard of '91' caused the deaths of 200 people in southern Britain. Over 6,000 farm animals froze to death and 63 ships were known to have been wrecked between the Goodwin Sands and the Isles of Scilly. With no thaw commencing until the 14, March, an average of 4 feet of snow blanketed Cornwall and Devon. In some areas the snow completely engulfed trains, no fewer than ten of which simply vanished under

drifts, their crew and passengers entombed in freezing conditions for up to four days before rescue. On Dartmoor the ravine known as Tavy Cleave, which is over 300 feet (nearly 100 metres) deep, was completely filled with driving snow right to the very top, and it was high summer 1891 before the last of the drifts melted!

What remains of the *Bay of Panama* today?

One hundred and twenty-eight years of winter gales and salvage work have reduced the remains of the ship to the level of the surrounding sand and rocks on which she lies. Made of steel, she has not been affected by teredo worm or other burrowing molluscs (unlike a wooden-hulled vessel), so the outline of her hull can still clearly be seen in the spring, before she becomes overgrown by seaweed. She lies in less than 30 feet (10 metres) of water, has no known owner and is not protected in any way.

In the Five Pilchards Inn, Porthallow, there are a number of relics from the wreck: a bronze rigging hawse, a piece of her original timber, a fine model of the ship in full sail and several photographs of the wreck itself. An anchor from the wreck stands on the foreshore as a poignant reminder of this terrible shipwreck.

SHIPWRECKED AT DINNER
LINER SS *Mohegan*

14 OCTOBER 1898 – MANACLE ROCKS, THE LIZARD

They say it's unlucky to change the name of a ship, and perhaps the loss of the *Mohegan* proves this superstition to be true? Originally one of four ships ordered by the Wilsons and Furness-Leyland Line, to be built by Earle's of Hull as luxury passenger liners and live animal carriers, she was to have been named *Cleopatra*. However, shortly before her launch the order was cancelled and on 29 July 1898 she was bought by the Atlantic Transport Company of London for £140,000. She proved an unlucky ship from the start. A strike delayed completion, and to avoid payment of a penalty in the purchase contract, she was put into service with numerous defects despite being classed A1 by Lloyd's. This was the highest classification which a ship could be given for insurance purposes by Lloyd's, whose survey would have been a meticulous examination of every aspect of her construction and fittings, so what went wrong is uncertain. However, on her maiden voyage to New York she leaked so badly during the Atlantic crossing, including the flooding of several state-cabins, that on arrival all return bookings were cancelled, and she sailed for London at half-speed carrying 600 cattle but no passengers, her crew short of seven seamen who had deserted.

Arriving in the Thames on 4 September 1898, she was towed to London's Royal Albert Docks where she underwent an extensive overhaul, and when work was completed on 5 October, she sailed for trials in the North Sea. After rigorous inspection by the Board of Trade, her classification of A1 at Lloyd's was renewed, only now the name on the Certificate of Seaworthiness was *Mohegan*. She sailed for Gravesend Reach on Thursday 13 October, going alongside to embark her 53 passengers for New York. With 103 officers and crew under Captain Richard Griffith, senior captain and Commodore of the Line, six cattlemen and one horseman (known as 'the cowboys of the sea'), she was carrying at least 156 people, though official records vary. She was in fact designed to carry 120 first class passengers only, with no second class or steerage, whilst below decks she was fitted with stalls for 700 live cattle.

The *Mohegan* anchored temporarily off Dover to drop off the Thames pilot, after which she proceeded down the Channel at 12 knots. At 2.30 p.m. on 14 October, when off Prawle Point, Devon, she signalled the Lloyd's Station, saying 'All well, report me', which would have been communicated by telegraph both to the ship's agent and the owners. It was suggested by the Coroner at the subsequent inquiry that the captain had interrupted the ship's passage by contacting Prawle Point, thus delaying their arrival

'in the dangerous waters of Falmouth Bay and the nearby Manacle Rocks.'

But this makes no sense, since the time taken to send a short message to the Signal Station by electric lamp in Morse code would have been negligible. Also, the waters of Falmouth Bay and the Manacles were no more dangerous than Portland Bill, Start or Prawle Point, and it is most unlikely that the ship would need to stop to make a relatively short signal lamp communication with the shore station.

As the *Mohegan* passed the Eddystone light off Plymouth, a fatal navigational error was made regarding her course. The Rame Head Coastguard noted she was ten miles offshore, at least seven miles closer in than they would expect with a liner. From there to clear the Lizard she would be expected to steer SW x W, but now the quartermaster was steering W x N, taking her towards the land and eventually to her demise. Who ordered or sanctioned this course will never be known, since all the deck officers were lost. Was it a misheard command between the captain and the quartermaster at the wheel, an error of plotting on her chart, a faulty compass, or was it deliberate? The overriding question is, why was the mistake not noticed or corrected by the duty watch officer, who would surely have looked at the main compass and checked their course at regular intervals?

As the *Mohegan* approached St Anthony Head, Falmouth, she should have been at least 15 miles further out to sea. Instead, she was now close inshore, heading at full speed in a straight line for the Helford River Estuary: her captain, watch officers and lookouts seemingly oblivious to the impending disaster. From Dodman Point onwards, had she been further offshore and where she was supposed to be, both fixed Lizard lights should have been seen, supposedly visible for 21 miles and certainly visible from south of the Manacles. It was Atlantic Transport Company policy to have three deck officers on the bridge for each watch whilst on passage through the English Channel. There were also two quartermasters, two seamen bridge lookouts and another in the crow's nest, 50 feet above the deck on the foremost of her four masts. With Captain Griffith on the bridge, there should have been nine pairs of eyes scanning the horizon for other vessels or danger, all of whom must have seen how close the shore lights of Falmouth town were to them. It is inexplicable that still no one on board commented.

Four people ashore saw the liner during the last few minutes of her short life: boatman Snell of the Falmouth Coastguards; Mr Fooks, Receiver of Wrecks at Falmouth; James Hill, coxswain of the Porthoustock lifeboat; and boatman Charles May of the Coverack Coastguards.

Each instinctively knew the ship was on the wrong course. The first to try to avert disaster was Charles May, who fired a rocket and lit blue warning flares. Coxswain Hill summoned his lifeboat crew with a maroon and his prompt action, taken even before the *Mohegan* was wrecked, saved many lives which otherwise would have been lost. Whether it was the rockets and flares that alerted the *Mohegan*'s crew to their predicament, or whether one of the bridge officers, realising the danger, ordered an emergency change of course, we will never know, but it was too late to save her.

As daylight was fading at about 6.45 p.m., just as the passengers were sitting down to dinner, the *Mohegan* slammed into the easternmost side of the Manacle Rocks. She struck first the Vase Rock, embedding her huge rudder, then ploughed into the Voices Rock followed by the three Maen Varses Rocks, tearing both her port and starboard sides wide open, and leaving her bow facing seaward. At first none of the passengers seemed to be aware of what to do, many remaining seated while the waiters continued to serve them dinner as if nothing untoward had happened, until a Charles Duncan jumped up from his table and shouted, 'to the Life Preservers'.

With no double bottom as modern ships have today, the engine-room immediately flooded to a depth of 14 feet. The ship's two electrical generators, which are clearly shown bolted down in the very bottom part of the ship in the original plans, were now underwater and ceased to work, plunging the ship into darkness. Today, electrical generators are always positioned much higher in ships, with additional stand-by emergency generators with secondary power sources as back-up. Additionally, there are normally emergency battery-operated lanterns throughout a ship, but no such facilities were available on the *Mohegan*.

With most of the passengers and some crew now on deck, Chief Officer Couch called for women and children to be saved first and ordered the lifeboats to be swung out. The *Mohegan* carried eight – six steel and two wooden – which between them could accommodate 284 people, but only if they could be launched. A complication then reared its ugly head. Captain Griffith had previously ordered the fitting of a second ship's railing, inboard of the lifeboats, 'to prevent the boats being rushed in an emergency', but when put to the test this served no purpose other than to impede the crew's attempts to lower them. This suggests that at no time was there a lifeboat drill either before or after the ship sailed, or this obstruction would have been obvious and possibly removed.

Within 12 minutes of hitting the Manacles, the ship was three parts underwater and, due to a heavy list to starboard of 40 degrees and the speed with which she went down, only two lifeboats got away, one of which capsized throwing its occupants into the sea. Many more might have been saved had everyone been wearing life-preservers, but these were mostly stowed below in lockers or cabins, now inaccessible, with only a small number on the upper deck near the boats. By dawn next day, only the *Mohegan*'s funnel and four masts showed above water.

Meanwhile, the Porthoustock lifeboat had already been launched, the crew rowing as hard as they could while Coxswain Hill burned white magnesium flares, hoping to attract the ship's lifeboats. Soon they encountered a mass of floating wreckage, then an upturned boat with four men clinging to the keel. As they took the survivors aboard, muffled cries were heard from beneath the capsized craft. After a considerable effort the lifeboat men managed to turn it over, to find two women alive, with a child and an adult male, both dead. One of the women, a Mrs Compton-Swift, had her left leg trapped, and that part of the boat had to be cut away with axes before she could be freed. She later told reporters there had been 25 occupants in the boat before it capsized, and that she had been trapped for over an hour. During the night the child had died of hypothermia, as had Charles Duncan, the passenger who had advised the others in the saloon to put on their life-preservers. The women said they could feel the drowned man's head bumping against them and were in despair, when suddenly the boat turned over and they were saved. The lifeboat coxswain then burnt three flares as a signal to the shore that more boats were required and continued to search for survivors, including some still clinging to the mizzen mast rigging. Eventually, after the arrival of the area's other lifeboats from Coverack, Cadgwith and Falmouth, 44 persons were saved, most of them by the Porthoustock lifeboat. The wreck of the *Mohegan* had taken with her 106 lives, including those of Captain Griffith and all the bridge officers.

Countless tales of heroism, suffering and bravery later emerged at the Board of Trade Inquiry, held at the Guildhall,

Westminster. But first there was a Coroner's inquest, which opened on 17 October 1898 in St Keverne village school hall, with Edward Laurence Carlyon presiding, the elected foreman of the jury being John Coad. The inquest concerned the 50 bodies brought ashore, of whom six were still registered as unidentified. It was established that 66 of the crew and 40 passengers had drowned or were missing, a total of 106. After questioning Alfred Williams, a representative of the *Mohegan*'s owners, Richard Kelly, a passenger and others, the inquest was adjourned, the Coroner explaining that a full Board of Trade inquiry would take place commencing on 11 November in London.

Amid concern at the large number of corpses now lying in St Keverne church, preparations were made for a mass burial. At the site originally chosen, rock prevented them from reaching the necessary depth, so an alternative site was chosen where a rectangular pit was dug measuring 19 x 13 x 10 feet deep (5.8 x 4 x 3 metres), with four additional private graves later. The 'Great Funeral', as it became known, took place on Wednesday 19 October, when 36 of the dead were buried in individual coffins stacked three deep. The Reverend Canon Diggens, assisted by the Reverend Dr Eajar and the Reverend Sell, conducted the service. Each coffin carried a wreath, lovingly made in St Keverne, but the grave was not completely back-filled in anticipation of further bodies being recovered. It was not fully closed until 11 November, the same day that the London inquiry opened. Eventually a granite monolith in the form of a traditional Celtic cross, designed by Plymouth architect Edmund Sedding, paid for in the most part by donations from St Keverne and the neighbourhood, was erected over the mass grave and dedicated. The base of the cross carries the one-word epitaph – 'Mohegan'.

There were many revelations and interesting accounts of events given at the inquiry. Quartermaster Juddery confirmed that when helmsmen were changed at the end of each watch, the course being steered was confirmed verbally, always witnessed by an officer. Juddery also confirmed that both second and third officers, Hindmarsh and Cole respectively, were the watch just before the ship struck, and that Able Seaman William Daniels, of Hastings, aged 33 and an experienced seaman, was the lookout in the crow's nest. The captain was heard to order as many women and children as possible to get into the jigger-masts rigging. Frank Nicklin, Chief Steward, confirmed that there were 30 stewards on board, who helped passengers put on their life-preservers, but that only two of his stewards survived. It was also suggested that there were two stowaways on board, an unidentified male who drowned and Daniel Gallaway, a black American. Daniel is said to have swum with two others to Coverack and survived, but there is no official record of this, only hearsay. In closing the inquiry, the court expressed its great approbation of the heroism of Mr Juddery, who swam from the wreck to the Porthoustock lifeboat, then back again with a line, by which all in the mizzen rigging were saved.

It is generally accepted that Captain Griffith went down with his ship, since his body was never recovered from the Manacles. It was later claimed that a headless body, said to have been wearing a sea captain's uniform jacket with rank insignia and brass buttons embossed ATL (the Company logo), was found three months after the wreck in Caernarvon Bay, Anglesey, but this has never been confirmed in any newspaper, burial register or coroner's inquest. It is inconceivable that a body could drift 250 miles from the wreck site, around the Lizard and Land's End and up the Welsh coast. However, an even more bizarre legend concerning Captain Griffith suggests that, as a shareholder of the Atlantic Transport Company, he deliberately lost his ship in order to claim a share of the insurance and that he escaped alive in the Porthoustock lifeboat and, on landing, ran up the beach and disappeared. The rumour was amplified by the sight of a stranger spotted rowing a boat across the Helford River to reach Falmouth, from where it would be possible to catch a train to Truro and thence to London, but no evidence has ever been produced to give credence to this story.

What remains of the *Mohegan* today?

The wreck lies at a depth of 75 feet (23 metres). There appear to be two ship's bells in existence, one carrying the name *Cleopatra*, the other *Mohegan*, but the latter is thought to be a fake. The *Cleopatra* bell, owned by the Roskilly family of St Keverne, is currently on display in the National Maritime Museum Cornwall, in Falmouth. The ship was heavily salvaged, though her four boilers survive amidst the wreckage, and St Keverne church has a memorial stained-glass window, as well as the cross over the mass grave. The Charlestown Shipwreck Centre has a large collection of her relics and fittings.

THE LOSS OF THE WORLD'S LARGEST SAILING SHIP SCHOONER *Thomas W. Lawson*

The world has seen many large sailing ships, barques, full-rigged ships and clippers, but none of them matched the sheer size of the American seven-masted schooner *Thomas W. Lawson*. Ten six-masted schooners had already been built at the time, and whilst steamships and sailing vessels of her tonnage would have carried a crew of at least 35, possibly as many as 50, the *Thomas W. Lawson* managed successfully with just 18 men! This was made possible by the foresight and ingenuity of a group of American businessmen led by a Thomas W. Lawson (1857–1925).

Lawson was one of America's richest men at the turn of the 20th century. He made and lost $60,000 before he was 17 and made $1 million before he was 21. As well as being a financier, Lawson was also a sailor, owning a massive yacht named *Dreamer*, which reflected the family estate known as Dreamworld, which became the most famous estate in America. As well as racetracks and stables, there were huge lakes and a flag pole 175 feet (53 metres) tall, flying the Stars and Stripes flag measuring 50 by 72 feet (15 x 22 metres).

To get from his estate at Sciatute to his waterfront office in Boston, he built his own railway station, connecting it to the Old Colony Railroad, and had a private train that ran non-stop for the 37 minutes it took to get him to work!

The contract to build the ship *Thomas W. Lawson* was signed in June 1901 by the Fore River Ship and Engine Company of Quincy, Massachusetts. Her frames and plating were all pre-formed, pre-punched and then riveted together, the holes matching exactly every time. She had two decks and six cavernous holds. Though entirely wind-powered, she had two engine-rooms, which provided steam to work her many winches. Apart from maintenance, no crew member was required to go aloft to set or furl sail, this being done mechanically from the main deck. Her lower masts were riveted steel, 32 inches (81 cms) in diameter, weighing 20 tons each. Her upper masts were made of pine. There was a telephone system between the wheelhouse and the two engine-rooms, the entire ship was lit by electricity, and steam heat kept the accommodation warm and provided unlimited hot water, a truly unique working environment for most seamen. She carried 25 sails, almost an acre of canvas, made in Gloucester, England.

The *Lawson*, as she was commonly known, was launched on 10 July 1902, having cost a quarter of a million dollars to build. She went into service hauling coal up and down the coast of the USA, but later became a bulk oil carrier, literally one of the first 'oil-tankers'. She proved to be a hard ship to handle; her high freeboard, her sheer weight and the seven masts with fore and aft rigging all meant any changes of course were difficult to manoeuvre. During early trials when her designer Mr Crowninshield was on board, he was asked 'How long will it take her to tack?' To which he replied, 'Go below, have your dinner, and when you get back she may, just may, be off on another tack!'

An unfortunate truth is that the *Thomas W. Lawson* was not well-designed. A small steam bow and stern thruster would have greatly assisted her to change course and manoeuvre, but these were not fitted. She is said to have run aground frequently due to her huge draft but, due to her excellent construction, never once leaked. When coal carrying became unprofitable by 1903, she was leased to the Sun Oil Company which fitted seven pairs of oil tanks, then all her topmasts were removed, her hollow main and upper masts now acting as oil vent tubes. This required reducing her sails from 25 to 10, and her previously white hull was now painted black.

In November 1907 the *Lawson* was prepared for her first transatlantic crossing, carrying a quarter of a million gallons of light oil in 58,000 barrels, loaded at Pennsylvania and destined for London. It had never been easy to find crew for the *Lawson*, and her last voyage saw her ready to sail under Captain George Dow with 18 crew, but two days before departure she lost six of them over a pay dispute. This meant that Captain Dow and First Mate Libby had to scour the waterfront to find replacements, those recruited being described as 'more warm-bodied than Able Seamen!'

They did not get off to an auspicious start, since the *Lawson* ran aground shortly after casting off and the tug *Paraguay* was employed to pull her off. She then cleared the Delaware River, and following a 'great-circle track' (the shortest distance between two points on the globe) for London at an average of 8 to 9 knots, the crossing should have taken around 15 days. Unfortunately, she encountered at least three gales with 90 mph winds, which shredded all but six of her sails and reduced three of her life-rafts to splinters. Her size alone contributed to the damage, her 404-foot (123-metre) long hull, weighing 10,860 tons, offering huge resistance to both wind and waves. Still, even under bare poles, she made 12 knots eastwards.

It was during the early afternoon of Friday 13 December that Captain Dow saw and recognised the Bishop Rock lighthouse, off the Isles of Scilly – but there was a serious problem. The *Lawson* should have passed it to port and well to the south, but the lighthouse was off to starboard and too close, meaning that she was driving into Broad Sound and shallow water. Fully appreciating his precarious position, Captain Dow ordered both two-ton bow anchors to be dropped, the port one having 900 feet (243 metres) of chain attached, the starboard anchor 540 feet (167 metres). Having seen the *Lawson*, the Bishop lighthouse-keepers fired a signal flare which was seen on St Agnes, where the pilots and boatmen knew only too well that there was a ship in trouble amid the Western Rocks.

Eleven men were already in the St Agnes lifeboat house by the time William 'Cook' Hicks (a Trinity House pilot) and his son Freddie arrived. The coxswain, William Mortimer, counted heads to find he had a full crew – two coxswains, ten oarsmen, and a bowman – and that they were ready for sea. All local volunteers, at least six of the crew were called Hicks and most related in some way. The coxswain ordered half the crew into the boat, while the rest pushed open the double doors of the lifeboat house, removed the chocks and pushed the boat out on its greased slipway. There was a heavy rolling sea coming in from the west, but they soon had the *Charles Deere James* afloat, a full crew aboard and the ten oars manned.

They steered and rowed south down Smith's Sound as far as Penny Ledges, then at the suggestion of the second coxswain, Abraham Hicks, and with the agreement of the first coxswain Mortimer, they turned and headed north for Annet Island Head. Twenty minutes later they were able to raise the lifeboat's sails, relieving the crew from the punishing task of rowing. Every man had already lashed himself down to his thwart to prevent him from being washed overboard as wave after wave struck the boat,

hurling green water and spume across its length. Somehow they got past Shark Fin Rock, then Old Wreck Rock and finally Jeffrey's Rock, the open Sound now in front of them.

As they approached the *Lawson*, it became obvious she was a wreck, not just another ship lying to her anchors. All her boats were smashed, the forecastle and poop deck structures had been torn away, the only sail she carried was in shreds and one of her holds had no covering. As they pulled alongside the sailing ship, Captain Dow showed his face.

'Captain, do you realise where you are and the dangerous position you are in?' asked Coxswain Mortimer.

'Oh, I'm all right,' Captain Dow responded. 'I have two anchors out and have ridden out worse storms than this.'

'Beg your pardon, sir, but you are not all right. I suggest you either get under way or else let my men take you and your crew to safety, on St Agnes,' suggested Mortimer.

'Have you a Trinity House pilot aboard?' asked Dow, to which the coxswain replied, 'Yes, we have, we'll sort one out and get him aboard.'

A discussion followed in the lifeboat as to who was going. Abraham Hicks, the second coxswain, was the next one due for what might be a very lucrative task, since if a pilot managed to save a ship there were huge potential rewards. But Abraham declined.

'All right, if you are not going then I will,' said Billy 'Cook' Hicks. 'Put the ladder over the side,' he shouted to Captain Dow.

Before he left, he suggested to the coxswain that the lifeboat lie astern of the *Lawson* on a heavy warp (a thick, heavy duty mooring rope); then he swung himself up the rope ladder and over the gunwhale to the *Lawson*'s main deck, where he addressed the captain, using the traditional question used when going aboard a ship:

'My name is Billy Hicks, sir, Trinity House pilot, permission to come aboard.'

Billy was escorted below decks to the captain's cabin where hot coffee was served and the situation discussed at length. Billy asked if the lifeboat crew, still floating astern, could be given a flask of coffee and some biscuits, which were gratefully received. A shout from the upper deck then advised that a second lifeboat was approaching. This was the St Mary's lifeboat *Henry Dundas*, whose coxswain asked Captain Dow the same questions put to him by the St Agnes lifeboat. His answers were the same:

'Thank you, but no thank you – we are staying here at anchor.'

The St Mary's boat passed under the stern of the *Lawson* in heavy seas, broke off her mizzen mast and suffered other damage, causing her to return to Hugh Town. Coxswain Mortimer then shouted for Billy Hicks to come to the stern, where he advised him that William Francis, one of the rowers, had collapsed in the bottom of the lifeboat, and he

felt he must return to St Agnes for medical assistance. The *Charles Deere James* left at 10 p.m. after Billy had reassured them that he would send up rockets if the situation deteriorated and he felt the lifeboat was required.

Back on St Agnes, the crew housed the lifeboat, leaving helpers to tidy it up, and after getting something to eat and a hot drink, retired to the St Agnes lighthouse lamp room, from where they could see the *Thomas W. Lawson*'s riding lights. At about 1.50 on the Saturday morning, Billy Hicks' son Freddie noticed that the lights were no longer visible. The men discussed what might have caused this, but any suggestion that they re-launch the lifeboat was vetoed due to the terrible sea conditions. They did not learn until the next day that, as the storm increased overnight to near-hurricane force, the *Lawson*'s anchor cables had both snapped at around 1.15 a.m. and the ship struck the rocks only 150 feet (45 metres) off Shag Rock, falling over to starboard before breaking in two. All seven masts had broken off and fallen into the sea, along with all the members of the crew, who had climbed the rigging for safety on the captain's command. Billy Hicks, who had lashed himself to the spanker mast rigging, the furthest aft of the seven masts, was catapulted out and never seen again.

At daybreak, the St Agnes lifeboat men resolved in desperation to return to the wreck, this time in one of their pilot gigs, a boat named *Slippen*. Seven men volunteered, the gig was launched at 7 a.m. and they rowed and sailed out to Shag Rock. Here they found the wreck upside down, the sea filled with drowned corpses, floating wreckage and a huge slick of mineral oil. The men landed on Annet Island where they found one of the *Lawson*'s seamen, George Allen, badly injured and screaming with pain, and took him back to St Agnes. At around noon the gig returned to look for more survivors and found Captain Dow and Edward Rowe, the senior engineer, in a crevice on Hellweathers Carn. They rescued Rowe first, taking him to St Agnes, then went back for Captain Dow. Freddie Hicks was the hero of this rescue, having swum the captain across a gully, then despite being half the other man's size, carried him hundreds of yards across slippery rocks to the gig. Both Dow and Rowe survived their ordeal, but George Allen succumbed to his injuries.

Despite every gallon of oil carried on board the *Lawson* escaping into the sea, which technically made it the world's first major maritime oil spill, it appears not to have affected the environment in any way and quickly dispersed, unlike the *Torrey Canyon* (pages 126 to 131), which carried crude oil. The 16 members of the crew of the *Lawson* who lost their lives were buried in an unmarked mass grave on St Agnes; Billy Hicks's body was never officially found, but a marker to him was erected around 2004. The crew of the *Slippen* gig received individual engraved gold medals from the American government for their heroism. Freddie Hicks received an engraved gold watch from Theodore Roosevelt, President of the United States, as well as a silver medal from the RNLI for his part in this tragic shipwreck. As for Thomas W. Lawson, the owner of the schooner, he eventually lost his fortune, his Dreamland estate was auctioned for unpaid taxes in 1922 and Lawson died relatively poor in 1925.

What remains of the *Thomas W. Lawson* today?
The remains of the ship still lie in two parts off Shag Rock in a depth of about 30 feet (10 metres), available for any diver to visit. In 2002, the American Scituate Historical Society and its Maritime and Irish Mossing Museum set up an exhibition devoted to the *Thomas W. Lawson*. With the help of Maggie Tucker and others on St Mary's who owned the gig *Slippen*, it was shipped on a cradle within a shipping container to the USA. The gig, built in 1870 and by then 133 years old, was shipped back in 2003 to Scilly. It is still used as a practice boat but no longer participates in the World Pilot Gig Championships. There are a range of artefacts in the St Mary's Museum and at least three books have been written about the incident, including Thomas Hall's *The T.W. Lawson – the Fate of the World's Only Seven-Masted Schooner* (The History Press, 2006).

THE ERA OF MODERN TECHNOLOGY
1914 - 2003

The 20th century witnessed unprecedented losses of both warships and merchant vessels in two World Wars, which occurred over a relatively short period of 11 years.

A total of 10,532 merchant vessels and warships were sunk, representing over 10 million tons of shipping. Three stories in this section, the loss of the British submarine *A-7* (pages 96 to 101), the German U-boat *U-66* (pages 108 to 113) and the achievements of the *U-21* (pages 102 to 107) were all part of the development of submarines, now accepted as the capital ship of the future. *U-21* sank over 40 ships, eight in one afternoon, as well as a Royal Navy cruiser and three battleships.

The loss of the 'Grand Old Lady', the battleship HMS *Warspite* (pages 114 to 119) in Mounts Bay, reflects the demise of 'floating gun-carriages', also the enormous increase in the size of modern ships and the unprecedented level of oil pollution tankers can create is portrayed in the wreck of the *Torrey Canyon* (pages 126 to 131), 61,236-tons, the largest tanker in the world at the time and the first major oil spill. Today, the *Pioneering Spirit*, 499,000-tons is the largest vessel afloat, the biggest ever built being the tanker *Seawise Giant* of 564,000-tons. The *Torrey Canyon*, the

Mont and the *Seawise Giant* were of different construction to earlier steel ships being of welded construction, not riveted, driven by diesel engines not steam and the latter, like all new tankers after 1975, had a double skinned hull.

The work of the Royal National Lifeboat Institution continues, and to this end its crews still put to sea in weather conditions sometimes so severe they are indescribable. The loss of the *Penlee* lifeboat (pages 132 to 141) whilst attempting to save the crew and passengers aboard the coaster MV *Union Star* and its tragic consequences are testimony to these brave souls and feature large in this section. By comparison, *RMS Mülheim* (pages 142 to 145) was lost in totally calm conditions, simply because the watch officer tripped, fell, and was knocked unconscious, an unfortunate twist of fate. Advances in technology including world-wide satellite communication, the Global Positioning System, accident black boxes on ships, better training and regulations have greatly reduced the number of shipwrecks. In 1856 an unbelievable 1,153 ships were wrecked on the UK coastline alone; 327 were wrecked worldwide in 1984 which by 2017 had dropped to 182, only two of which were in the UK , weather still the predominant cause.

THE TRAGIC LOSS OF ELEVEN ROYAL NAVY SUBMARINERS
HM SUBMARINE *A7*

Two Royal Navy submarines in line astern, each proudly flying the white ensign, slowly made their way from the River Tamar and through the narrows between Drake's Island and Devil's Point, Stonehouse. They made for a grand gesture, being part of the largest navy in the world at the time; early-morning walkers on Plymouth Hoe stopped to watch them with pride as they entered Plymouth Sound heading towards the western end of the breakwater. The storm clouds of war were already gathering over Europe and the sight of the two submarines, led by the depot ship HMS *Onyx* (formerly a torpedo gunboat) and her tender HMS *Pygmy*, going about their business offered reassurance to those who were watching that the Royal Navy would keep Britain safe. It was 16 January 1914.

The conning towers of the small early A-Class submarines were little more than open platforms, holding a brass steering wheel similar to that of a motor vehicle, mounted flat on top of a vertical control shaft. Forward of the steering position were a couple of tall ventilators, the conning tower entry hatch and then the periscope, which was a permanent fixture, incapable of retraction. On *A7*, directly in line behind *A9* in the flotilla, the coxswain Petty Officer Crowley was at the helm, taking orders from Lieutenant Gilbert Molesworth Welman RN, with his First Lieutenant and navigator, Sub-Lieutenant Robert Herman Grant Morrison RN close at hand. A few feet further forward, Able Seaman Charles Russell stood look-out, half in and half out of the circular hatch leading down into the body of the submarine, his feet on the access ladder. Lieutenant Welman, who was technically captain of the boat, had the official title of Lieutenant and Commander, whilst Sub-Lieutenant Morrison was designated First Lieutenant and Executive Officer.

Since it was only 7.45 a.m., the sun had yet to show itself above the horizon, but the day looked promising: the weather being fine and clear, the wind a gentle breeze from the south-west. The crew of *A7* were looking forward to a quiet day at sea firing practice torpedoes at their Torpedo

Boat escorts, before returning to Devonport before dark. Lieutenant Welman, aged 26, a Cornishman from Newquay, who had commanded *A7* for only two months, was probably telling his junior officer of the plans for his forthcoming marriage to Miss Enid Russell Brown in the near future.

Unlike modern submarines, the tiny 180-ton A-Class boats were open inside from end to end, with no bulkheads (hence no watertight compartments), the interior literally an open space from stern tube to her two forward torpedo tubes. It was also a very cramped class of submarine with not a spare inch of space. During the design phase, Captain Reginald Bacon, Inspecting Captain of Submarines, had ordered the removal of all unnecessary brackets, fittings and even grab rails to ensure that the finished boat was actually light enough to float! Designated by the Admiralty as Coastal Patrol Boats, there were no officers' cabins, bunks or galley, not even a head (toilet), the crew literally sharing a bucket. Designed for day patrols only, the crew lived on bully-beef sandwiches, biscuits and tea when at sea.

Senior officers in our Edwardian Royal Navy were still divided in their attitude to submarines. The old brigade was unwilling to accept that their battleships, those ponderous expensive floating gun-carriages, were redundant, and that the submarine was the capital ship of the future. They even described them as

> '*an underhand form of warfare, and a damned un English weapon!*'

Even the Comptroller of the Navy stated that

> '*submarines would never be any use in war*'.

How wrong they were! But their attitude meant that our submarine development was slow, and the Vickers shipyard at Barrow-in-Furness built only 13 of these early A-Class boats between 1902 and 1905, before constructing more advanced B- and C-Class boats.

Astern of the 'control area' of *A7* was her single Wolseley 16-cylinder, 500-brake-horsepower petrol engine, used only when the boat was surface-running, making her capable of 12 knots. Once submerged, a 150-hp electric motor fed by a large bank of built-in lead-acid batteries made her capable of 8 knots, the batteries being recharged whilst surface-running. In charge of propulsion was Chief Petty Officer First Class Engine-Room Artificer (ERA) Richard Venning (43), a temporary replacement covering for the boat's regular Chief ERA who was ashore sick. His three assistants were Petty Officer Second Class ERA Robert Nagle (35) and Acting Leading Stokers, John Northam (32) and Lancelot Wagstaff (25).

The other four crew members were all Able Seamen: Ernest Dyer, Frank Harris, Frederick Jewell (another temporary replacement) and Charles Russell, who were probably sitting on the portable canvas stools which the boat carried. Of the 11 men aboard *A7*, five were married with a total of six children between them. There were in addition three other unusual little lives on board – three white mice in a cage. Mice were carried on board all British submarines fitted with petrol engines at the time and were there to detect carbon monoxide, since they would keel over if levels became too high, long before humans would be affected. Despite the hazards of petrol fumes, the cramped conditions and the ever-present danger of flooding, men were more than willing to volunteer for this new submarine service. There was of course the incentive of 'hard-lying' money, six shillings a day for officers and two shillings for able seamen, intended to compensate for the primitive conditions in which they were expected to work.

On leaving Plymouth Sound, *A9* took up a position 2½ miles (about 4 kms) WNW of Rame Head and commenced a series of 'attacks' on *Pygmy*. Once her two spent practice torpedoes, which incidentally cost £1,000 each, were recovered, it was *A7*'s turn to follow suit. She was supposed to have been on the same bearing from Rame Head 2 miles (3.2 kms) further out to sea, but was seen by *Pygmy*'s lookouts, trimmed down and ready to dive but a further 2 miles SE of where she should have been. By 11 a.m. *A7* had dived and *Pygmy* commenced her run, but when no 'attack' appeared to have been made, she awaited *A7*'s surfacing ready to make a second 'attack'; but *A7* never reappeared.

Pygmy then steamed towards Rame Head searching for the missing submarine, at the same time showing a black ball at her yardarm as a signal for *A7* to surface immediately. The time was 11.55 a.m. At 12.15 p.m. her lookouts spotted a huge disturbance on the surface and three minutes later a second disturbance, as if a large amount of compressed air

had been discharged underwater. Reaching the spot, *Pygmy* dropped a surface marker buoy 3 miles (4.8 kms) W by N from Rame church, then at maximum speed returned to Devonport to report the incident to the Commander-in-Chief on board the submarine depot ship *Forth*, there being no radio communication between the ships.

Despite a buoy marking the approximate position of *A7*'s disappearance, it took six days of sweeping with a wire slung between two ships before she was located on 22 January, *Pygmy* now reporting oil floating on the surface. Royal Navy copper-helmeted standard divers went down and found the submarine in 121 feet (37 metres) depth, with some 20 to 22 feet (6 to 7 metres) of her stern buried deep in the seabed. The rest of *A7*'s hull, approximately 78 feet (25 metres) long, was sticking up at an angle of 30°, her bow some 33 feet (10 metres) clear of the bottom. The divers tapped all around the hull with the handles of their diving knives, hoping for a response, but the wreck remained ominously silent. On 26 January efforts to pull *A7* out of her grave were unsuccessful due to bad weather. It was 28 January before a 5½-inch (14-cm) hawser was shackled to an eye-plate on the submarine's bow, the other end taken on board the 14,000-ton battleship *Exmouth* whose massive capstans exerted a huge pulling power. But all that happened when the battleship took the strain was for the eye-plate to fracture, leaving *A7* as they had found her.

It was not until 17 February that attempts at salvage resumed. This time a 6½-inch (16.5-cm) hawser was placed around the wreck but under strain it slipped free, and a similar attempt eight days later also failed. Doubts were now being cast on the feasibility of ever raising her. On 27 February, a further attempt failed, and the combined prospects of further bad weather and the difficulties of raising the wreck from the depth of 120 feet caused the operation to be abandoned. *A7*, with her crew of 11 still inside, was written off.

In hindsight it is understandable but at the same time remarkable that the Admiralty salvage teams gave up so easily. On 10 December 1913, 37 days prior to the disappearance of *A7*, the Royal Navy submarine *C14* had sunk between Drake's Island and Devil's Point in approximately 100 feet (30 metres) of water. She was on passage from Portsmouth to Plymouth with other submarines of the 3rd Flotilla, when in the narrows between Drake's Island and the mainland she was in collision with HM Hopper barge *No. 27*. Damage to her port quarter caused the submarine to flood, and despite collision mats being placed over the hole by the crew she filled and sank. Fortunately, her crew of 19, including her commanding officer Lieutenant G.W. Naper, RN, escaped without loss of life or injury. Within seven days the submarine was raised, dry-docked, and eventually served for a further eight years. A specially designed Salvage Lighter *No. 94* had made this possible; with hawsers being positioned under the wreck and using what is called a 'tidal lift', she was successfully brought to the surface.

If *C14* could be raised so easily and quickly, why was the same technique and salvage barge not used on *A7*? The former, *C14*, which was larger and heavier, sank in a similar depth but in sheltered waters with every dockyard facility at hand, whereas *A7* was in the open sea, exposed to winter gales, with a third of her hull deeply embedded in the seabed. Since she lay sticking up at an angle, hawsers placed around the submarine forward of the conning tower were prone to slip off, while those aft of the conning tower were attempting to lift both the 180-tons of vessel and an indeterminate weight caused by her entrapment. A grab dredger would have been capable of removing sufficient seabed material to release her stern, but in winter sea conditions this would have been impossible. Which leaves the question, why was *A7* unable to resurface after her first dive?

The 1914 divers found her bow torpedo doors, torpedo loading hatch and the conning tower hatch fully shut, which suggests there was no accidental flooding. Flooding may have occurred if any fitting, valve or seal had leaked but *A7* had been in service for nine years and any such component failures would have already shown. We know she was not in collision, since on the day she was lost Whitsand Bay was closely monitored by HMS *Onyx* and *Pygmy*. That leaves the possibility of asphyxiation of the crew by petrol fumes, but since *A7* was slightly positively buoyant, if the crew had become unconscious the submarine would have floated to the surface unaided.

The most likely explanation is that she became difficult to control as she dived, which was a known trait of A-Class boats. Her stern may have ploughed into the seabed, and if her electric motor was running ahead at the same time she could have blasted a hole in the seabed into which she slipped even further, which then caved in trapping her. Further attempts to use her propeller would only have exacerbated the problem, until eventually her propeller would have stalled her engine. The released air seen on the surface was most likely the crew's attempt to blow out her water ballast, resulting in her bow being raised at an angle whilst her stern remained embedded. This may have drained her batteries and without power she would have been helpless. The crew would have survived for as long as the remaining air was breathable, after which they would have slipped into unconsciousness and died peacefully of carbon dioxide (CO_2) poisoning. We will probably never know exactly why *A7* ended up stuck in the seabed, or the circumstances causing the death of her crew.

The A-Class submarines were not the first of the Royal Navy's 'British-built' boats, since they followed the Holland Class, an American-designed and built submarine of which Great Britain eventually had five. Seven A-Class boats, out of the total of 13 built, were lost between 1904 and 1917, the causes ranging from collision, explosion and human error, to simply unknown.

What remains of Submarine *A7* today?

Nothing of the *A7* can be seen today unless you are a diver. The site where she lies is 8 nautical miles (15 kms) from Sutton Harbour in Plymouth, at a depth of 121 feet (37 metres) plus the height of the tide. The submarine has been a Designated War Grave since 2002, which means that permission is required to dive the wreck. A recent survey by the Plymouth-based SHIPS Project (Shipwrecks and History In Plymouth Sound) found her now lying flat on the seabed, upright with roughly two-thirds of her hull buried in silt. The compass binnacle mounted on the deck astern of the conning tower is now at the Submarine Museum, Gosport, minus its iron correction spheres. The 'bridge' telegraph has been removed at some point by divers, as has her port side navigation light. The periscope is bent backwards at approximately 30°, and at some point divers have attempted to remove it by cutting through it just above its support collar. The glass of the two scuttles in the main conning tower hatch are both broken. Her pressure hull is undamaged apart from three small holes probably caused by corrosion, and it is believed that there is minimal mud silting inside the hull itself.

BETRAYED – SEVEN NEUTRAL SHIPS SUNK IN AN AFTERNOON

SS *Bandoeng*, SS *Eemland*, SS *Gaasterland*, SS *Jacatra*, SS *Noorderdijk*, SS *Zaandijk* & SS *Normanna*

22 FEBRUARY 1917 – NORTH-WEST OF THE ISLES OF SCILLY

By 1917 both the Admiralty and the British government had learnt two hard lessons: first, that submarines, rather than lumbering great battleships and huge fleets, were the capital ships of the future; and second, that the German use of submarines to sink merchant ships with the aim of starving Britain into submission was succeeding. By January of that year, less than two and a half years into WW1, U-boats had sunk 637 British-registered as well as 1,096 Allied or neutral merchant ships, a total of 1,733 cargo-carrying vessels, representing 300,000 tons a month. If the war were to continue and if the hoped-for entry of the United States into the war on the side of the Allies did not materialise, ship losses on this scale were unsustainable and Great Britain would eventually be forced to surrender.

Cornwall's contribution to the U-boat war was considerable, with Royal Navy Auxiliary Patrol Stations (RNAPS) at both Falmouth and St Mary's in the Isles of Scilly. There were also four Royal Naval Air Stations (RNAS) around the coast, including one at Tresco on Scilly, as well as dozens of armed trawlers, drifters and yachts. These ships were hunting and attacking submarines, escorting merchant vessels, towing damaged ships or picking up survivors, mine-sweeping and mine-laying, while the seaplanes and airships were escorting individual ships or spotting and attacking U-boats from the air.

Between October 1916 and January 1917, seven independent neutral Dutch merchant ships were stopped in the English Channel by Royal Navy warships and ordered into Falmouth, so that their cargoes could be examined for contraband. Once cleared, the British authorities refused them permission to put to sea on the grounds that they were bound to be sunk by German U-boats, so they had no choice but to remain at anchor in the Carrick Roads. Their owners then pressed the Dutch government to approach Germany for immunity from attack, and eventually each vessel received a letter granting them a safe passage. Before they left Falmouth, all seven ships were painted in the new dazzle camouflage being used extensively on British merchant and warships alike. This broke up their outline at sea, making it more difficult for U-boat commanders to determine where to aim their torpedoes. At the same time each ship's name in huge letters and the Dutch flag was painted on each side, establishing their identity and nationality from a distance. Why the authorities had them dazzle-camouflaged to make it more difficult for submarine commanders to see them, then painted a huge neutral Dutch flag on their sides, is inexplicable.

Although they sailed from Falmouth at the same time and remained within sight of each other, they were not a 'convoy' as such since they had several different destinations. Neither were they afforded any warship protection, which was unfortunate as otherwise they would probably have survived. They took the route between the Seven Stones Reef and Land's End and, when north of Scilly, headed west. Only one of the Dutch vessels, the 3,770-ton SS *Eemland*, was on direct passage for New York; the 3,917-ton SS *Gaasterland* and the 4189-ton SS *Zaandijk*, the latter carrying ballast, were heading for New Jersey and Philadelphia respectively. Four other ships – the 5,851-ton SS *Bandoeng*, carrying Java produce, the 5,373-ton SS *Jacatra* and the 5874-ton SS *Menado*, all from Batavia in the Dutch East Indies, and the 7,166-ton SS *Noorderdijk*, laden with cornmeal and wheat – were en route for Rotterdam, intending to leave the 'convoy' and proceed around the north of Scotland to reach their destination. The seven ships reached the same area north-west of the Bishop Rock at much the same time and were still within sight of Scilly when, by total chance, they encountered the German submarine *U-21*.

SM *U-21* and her charismatic commander, *Kapitänleutnant* Otto Hersing, a tall, slender, sullen seaman of vast experience, were heroes of the German *Kaiserliche Marine* (Imperial Navy) in the eyes of the German population. Only 32 days after Great Britain had declared war on Germany, on 5 September 1914 Hersing torpedoed the Scout-class 2940-ton cruiser HMS *Pathfinder* off St Abb's Head in the North Sea. She sank in four minutes killing 259 of her crew, the first warship ever to be sunk by a submarine. Lieutenant Commander Otto Hersing and *U-21* were already making history!

In April 1915, Hersing was ordered to transfer to the eastern Mediterranean to support Germany's allies the Ottoman Empire, under attack from British and French troops at the Dardanelles. SM *U-21* arrived off Pola in early May and by the end of the month and within three days of each other, she had torpedoed and sunk HMS *Triumph* and HMS *Majestic*, both battleships, the former on 25 May off Gallipoli, the latter on 27 May off Cape Helles. The troops on the steep coastal hillside overlooking the scene actually stopped fighting just to watch the spectacle, as the *Triumph* slowly capsized close inshore. Her masts and funnels tilted over until they touched the sea; her torpedo booms, draped with now useless nets, pointed to the sky; then she turned over completely and sank. Hersing's successes in the eastern Mediterranean forced the Allies to withdraw all their shipping from Cape Helles and on 5 June he received the 'Pour le Mérite' award, the highest

German military honour, equivalent to our Victoria Cross. The *U-21* also torpedoed the French cruiser *Carthage* on 4 July off Turkey. No wonder that in German naval circles Hersing became known as the '*Zerstörer von Schlachtschiffe*' (destroyer of battleships).

Further sinkings followed throughout 1916, totalling 12 ships amounting to 24,000 tons overall. These included the British steamer SS *Belle of France* and the French armoured cruiser *Amiral Charner*, both in February 1916, the SS *City of Lucknow* off Malta in April, and the steamship SS *Glenlogan* in October. In December *U-21* torpedoed the SS *Benalder* east of Crete, but though severely damaged the ship managed to reach Alexandria. At the beginning of 1917, SM *U-21* left the Mediterranean to support the unrestricted submarine warfare campaign being promoted by the *Seekriegsleitung* (Maritime Warfare Command). On her way north, she intercepted and sank two British merchant ships and two smaller Portuguese vessels off the coast of Portugal, followed by the French freighter *Cacique* (2,917 tons) in the Bay of Biscay, and was just approaching the Irish Sea when the seven Dutch ships came into sight.

It is not clear whether the safe passage promised to the neutral Dutch merchant ships had not been communicated to *U-21*, or if Hersing feigned ignorance of the agreement. At any rate, Hersing showed them no mercy and sank all but one over the course of a single day, like ducks at a fairground shooting gallery. The SS *Bandoeng* was the first to be torpedoed, followed by the *Jacatra* and the *Noorderdijk*; having run out of torpedoes by this time, the crew of SM

U-21 boarded the other vessels and planted explosives which when detonated caused them to sink. Only on the SS *Menado* did the explosive charges fail to detonate completely and though damaged, the ship did manage to reach port. Whilst thus engaged, the *U-21* was presented with another target in the form of the 2,900-ton Norwegian steamer *Normanna*, carrying phosphate from Savannah to Stavanger. Although, like the Netherlands, Norway was officially neutral in WW1, the *Normanna* met the same fate as the Dutch ships and was scuttled.

In every case however, the crews were given time to abandon ship in their own boats, and not a single life was lost. As the lifeboats approached the Isles of Scilly they were seen by the Bishop Rock lighthouse keepers, who reported them to the C.O. of the Naval Base at St Mary's. As a result the St Agnes lifeboat, the *Charles Deere James*, went to their assistance, whilst several armed trawlers and the packet steamer *Lyonesse* put to sea to search for more survivors. With over 500 seamen landing on St Mary's quay in 24 hours, armed guards were employed in escorting them to the Town Hall to stop local inhabitants from talking to them, since security was considered important. At the Town Hall they were given hot drinks and food, then Royal Naval personnel recorded their identities and ranks, which ship they had been on, next-of-kin and so on. The SS *Lyonesse*, which operated the packet mail service between the islands and Penzance, was kept busy for several days shipping the rescued crews to the mainland, where trains conveyed them to London, and from there back to Holland. Having reneged on its promise of free passage, the German

SS *BANDOENG*, SS *EEMLAND*, SS *GAASTERLAND*, SS *JACATRA*, SS *NOORDERDIJK*, SS *ZAANDIJK* AND SS *NORMANNA* government was forced to compensate the owners of the Dutch ships.

The Netherlands' section of the League of Neutral Countries awarded a special medal to each member of the St Agnes lifeboat, as well as to the crews of the armed trawlers that had rescued survivors. These were presented on St Mary's by Mrs Dorrien-Smith of Tresco, the wife of the Lord Proprietor of the Isles of Scilly.

Whilst over 100 ships were sunk around the Isles of Scilly in World War 1, the loss of seven ships in an afternoon together with the survival of every single man aboard set a record. As for *Kapitänleutnant* Otto Hersing, by the end of WW1 he had been responsible for the sinking of 40 ships, amounting to over 113,000 tons, making him one of the most victorious commanders of the *Kaiserliche Marine*. His submarine *U-21* surrendered after the Armistice but accidentally sank in the North Sea whilst under tow of a British warship on 22 February 1919, exactly two years after her most successful, and destructive, day. Hersing retired from active service after the war and surprisingly, given his glorious naval career, became a potato farmer. He died on 5 July 1960, aged 74.

What remains of this incident?
The seven sunken ships still lie in some 60 fathoms of water in the Western Approaches. As no lives were lost in the sinking of these ships, no plaque exists on the Isles of Scilly to commemorate the event. Unless some relic of the *U-21* remains in Germany, the entire incident has passed into history.

A Dutch merchant ship circa 1917.

SS *BANDOENG*, SS *EEMLAND*, SS *GAASTERLAND*, SS *JACATRA*, SS *NOORDERDIJK*, SS *ZAANDIJK* AND SS *NORMANNA*

SUNK BY A FLYING BOAT

SUBMARINE *UC-66*

When Great Britain declared war on Germany and Austria in 1914, it appears that few in government were aware of how inadequately prepared the country was for war, particularly a war at sea. The Royal Navy was still the largest in the world, and the government seems to have believed, complacently, that its sheer size was sufficient to defend the nation and keep open the trade routes with the still vast British Empire. Our Admirals, with few exceptions, had an even more unfortunate mind-set, being unwilling to consider that either submarines or aircraft could play a major role in war. They even rejected the offer from the American Wright brothers to use their aircraft patents, saying that

'Their Lordships can see no use for aircraft by the Royal Navy'![1]

After all, we had the largest fleet of 'floating gun-carriages' (battleships) in the world, which had remained unchallenged since Trafalgar. What the Royal Navy was desperately short of was anti-submarine vessels, and to this end 150 deep-sea fishing vessels were requisitioned on 4 August 1914, the day war was declared. These were immediately taken into naval dockyards for conversion, where their fish-holds were turned into accommodation and they were armed with deck guns, painted grey and given pennant numbers, before being commissioned into the Royal Navy and sent to war.

To our cost, the Admiralty initially ignored the fact that as an island nation we were dependent on a regular supply of food and raw materials brought in by sea, and that if the supply lines were cut we would eventually be starved into submission. In the previous chapter, we have already seen the havoc which could be wreaked on shipping by one U-boat alone. In 1915, German U-boats sank 774 ships worldwide. This figure doubled to 1,823 in 1916 and 1917 saw a huge increase to 3,209, of which 2,895 were allied vessels and 314 neutral. The threat to supplies was greatly increased by the practice of allowing merchant ships to sail

[1] Quoted in M J Trow, *The Isle of Wight in the Great War* (Pen & Sword Books, 2015)

alone instead of in protected convoys. Despite proposals from the British War Cabinet early in 1917, the Admiralty continued to resist pressure to provide armed warships as escorts for convoys until mounting losses of ships and their cargoes caused Britain's grain reserves to dwindle to six weeks' supply, meaning that food rationing would need to be introduced.

The sheer numbers of ships lost to U-boat action created a problem which could only be partly offset by the help that American and Canadian shipyards were prepared to offer. To put it into perspective, at a time when ships built in Europe were still riveted, it took at least a year to complete a 10,000-ton merchant ship; therefore, replacing the 3,209 ships sunk in 1917 would take 100 shipyards over 32 years!

Although the Isles of Scilly, with only 2,000 inhabitants and limited contact with the mainland, were of low priority to the War Department in 1914, they came to play a hugely important role in the Western Approaches submarine war from 1915 onwards. There were 21 armed trawlers and drifters at St Mary's, where a base of the Royal Navy Auxiliary Patrol Service (specifically for anti-submarine purposes) was established in 1915, and 14 mixed flying boats and seaplanes at the Royal Naval Air Station (RNAS) base at New Grimsby on Tresco, operational from early 1917 onwards. The number of naval personnel on the islands (around 1,500 overall) almost matched that of the resident population. The sheer presence of armed trawlers carrying 12-pounder guns and, later, depth-charges, made German U-boats cautious about surfacing to look for ships:

sonar (underwater sound navigation system) was still in the early stages of development and not available to German submarines at the time, so regular 'porpoising' (alternately rising and submerging) was necessary just to find targets. If an enemy submarine was spotted surfacing, the location was radioed to the naval headquarters on Scilly, and armed trawlers, drifters or patrol launches in the area would converge, whilst overhead patrolling airships or flying boats would be ready to swoop down and bomb without warning.

One such incident took place in April 1917 and another, which made aviation history, a month later. The aircraft in use were American Curtiss Model H-12s, twin-engine bi-planes which were the favoured workhorses on Tresco, carrying a crew of four and a 400-lb bomb load. On 27 April 1917, Curtiss H-12 flying boat No. 8654 was on a routine patrol north-west of Tresco, when her crew sighted a German U-boat on the surface. The U-boat chose not to dive as the aircraft approached but instead fought back, machine-gun fire from her conning tower raking and disabling the aircraft so that it could not drop its bombs, forcing it to return to base. But the second incident was both dramatic and, as far as the British were concerned, successful, being the only occasion during WW1 when a German submarine was sunk by an aircraft.

The morning of 27 May 1917 dawned bright and clear on the Isles of Scilly following a period of unsettled weather. Tresco Channel, the flying boats' 'runway', was flat calm, making for ideal flying conditions. At 8 a.m., the duty ground crew put their shoulders to the two huge hangar doors on Tresco's waterfront, rolling them open on their steel tracks. They then set about completing their aircraft's D.I (Daily Inspection). There were ten flying boats and seaplanes in the hangar all sitting on their launch trolleys, some already being worked on. The ground crew carefully pushed H-12 (No. 8656) out onto the concrete hard standing and into the sunlight. Fuel and radio checks completed, a Chief Aircraft Artificer climbed into the open cockpit to operate the controls and signalled to the ground crew that he was ready to start the port engine. This required a rating to climb onto the lower wing, grasp a blade of the four-bladed wooden propeller and swing it round until the petrol engine fired. The same procedure saw the starboard engine up and running. and only when the instrument readings of temperature, pressure, fuel and revolutions were acceptable were both engines shut down. Then the armourers took over, loading four 100-lb (45-kg) bombs onto the underslung bomb racks, two on each side, a thin wire attached to each bomb's tail fuze connected to the aircraft.

By now the aircrew had arrived, dressed in their uniform of sheepskin-lined leather flying jackets, helmets and lambswool leggings, their hands protected by leather gauntlets. The pilot, Flight Lieutenant Hoare RN, and his co-pilot, Flight Lieutenant Anderson RN, greeted Chief Petty Officer Artificer Tadman, the aircraft's flight engineer, and their wireless operator, Naval Airman Roy Chapman, with whom they had flown many times. The aircraft was pushed to the head of the concrete slipway where the crew boarded; then, still on its launch trolley, the aircraft rolled down into the sea where its engines were started. Satisfied

with the instrument readings and the wireless operator's 'thumbs up', indicating that Tresco Flying Control had given permission to take off, the pilots taxied out past Big Rock to Queen's Ledge, then turned to face north-west. The length of Tresco Channel was now open in front of them with only a slight surface chop and, as the aircraft picked up speed and commenced to lift, so the peace and tranquillity of the Channel was shattered by two 275-hp Rolls-Royce Eagle 1 aero-engines at full power. Hangman's Island flashed by to port, then Cromwell's Castle to starboard until, off Little Kettle Rock, the flying boat became airborne. With the sun behind them and a clear horizon, they climbed to 1,500 feet (455 metres), then levelled out, heading 300° in Patrol Area III working seaward to the area identified as Box T8, which would take them some 90 miles (144 kms) away from Scilly at its extremity.

All four crew, who were wearing flying goggles, were scanning the sea ahead and off to each side for the tell-tale finger and wake of a submarine's periscope breaking the surface. Chapman, the wireless operator, then received an urgent message that one of the patrol trawlers had sighted a U-boat on the surface off to starboard of their present course. Lieutenant Hoare was passed a hand-scribbled pencil message on a signal pad; he immediately changed course and dropped down to 500 feet (150 metres). Suddenly, there right in front of them was a surfaced German UC-class mine-layer submarine – and the aircraft had only been airborne for 15 minutes!

Approaching from astern of the enemy, its engines throttled

back to reduce their noise, the aircraft was not immediately seen, but as they levelled out for a copy-book bombing run, a Spandau machine gun on the submarine's conning tower opened fire at them and soon tracer rounds could be seen punching holes in the flying boat's upper and lower wings. The aircraft roared low over the U-boat only some 300 feet (90 metres) up. When directly over the U-boat, the co-pilot Anderson pulled both the port and starboard bomb release levers and her four 100-lb high-explosive bombs fell away. With the fuse pins pulled out by their wires and the fuze propellers spinning to arm the bombs, after initially wobbling in flight until their tail fins steadied their descent, all four hit the U-boat's outer hull casing just forward of her conning tower and exploded. As the flying boat pulled out of its attack and turned to port, the aircrew had a grandstand view of the bombs detonating, throwing great columns of smoke and seawater into the air, leaking oil already spreading out across the surface. They were still taking machine gun-fire, but this then ceased as the stern of the submarine rose clean out of the sea at an angle of 60°, her two bronze propellers still turning. It was obvious that the bombs had caused the forepart of the submarine to flood, the weight of water pouring in pushing her bow ever deeper, until her stern was almost vertical She then slid gracefully down towards the seabed and a watery grave with all 23 of her crew, since no survivors were seen or found by the armed trawlers which raced to the scene, only a great patch of light oil marking the spot.

Chapman was reporting their action by wireless back to Tresco, when Flight Engineer Tadman became aware that glycol cooling fluid was pouring out from the starboard engine radiator, having been ruptured by a bullet. Realising this could cause the engine to overheat and seize, Tadman undid his safety harness, took off his gauntlets and without a thought for his personal safety, climbed out onto the lower starboard wing where he wrapped one arm round a bracing strut, whilst with his right hand he pulled a handkerchief out of his trouser pocket. This he forced into the hole, pushing it as tight as possible to stop the leak. With co-pilot Anderson carefully watching the engineer and making hand signals of encouragement to hang on, Lieutenant Hoare turned the aircraft back towards New Grimsby Sound and their Tresco base, which was still over 20 minutes' flying time away. Tadman, severely buffeted by the wind, the engine exhaust and the slip-stream of some 90 mph, and unable to let go either of the brace or his handkerchief, somehow remained there for over 45 minutes in total until they landed and taxied back to the launch slipway. Only then could the pilot stop both engines, allowing Tadman to slump down on the upper surface of the wing, exhausted and frozen.

As this proved to be the only U-boat to be sunk by an aircraft during the entire war, each member of the flying boat's crew received gallantry medals and Chief Petty Officer Tadman was hailed as a national hero for his impromptu action. Both pilots were awarded the Distinguished Service Cross (DSC), Tadman received a Conspicuous Gallantry Medal (CGM) and Wireless Operator Chapman a Distinguished Service Medal (DSM). It was later discovered that the aircraft had been hit by eight bullets from the U-boat. Only then was it revealed that Tadman had been the artificer responsible for solving an earlier bomb release mechanism problem. The flexible Bowden cables running from the cockpit that released bombs on all seaplanes were found to be suffering serious salt water corrosion. In his spare time at his lodgings on St Mary's, Tadman worked out a solution and made a drawing of a steel replacement mechanism for the cables. He paid a local blacksmith to make the rough parts in his forge and case-harden them, and then finished off the mechanism by hand himself in the Tresco workshops. This was so effective that it solved the problem completely, and the modification was adopted on all aircraft throughout the Royal Naval Air Service.

Flight Lieutenant William Anderson RN was quite a remarkable man. He had served throughout WW1, initially in the 1st King Edward's Horse cavalry regiment, before transferring to the RNAS in 1915 and then in 1918 to the newly-formed RAF. A very sensitive and religious man, he became very depressed over his part in being responsible for the deaths of the entire crew of the submarine. He underwent extensive psychiatric treatment and after being demobbed he took Holy Orders, becoming ordained as a priest in 1921. For a while he re-joined the Royal Navy as a chaplain, then went on to become the Bishop successively of Croydon, Portsmouth and finally Salisbury. He is believed to hold the unique distinction of being the only bishop to have served in all three of the armed forces. His co-pilot Flight Lieutenant Robin Hoare performed further acts of gallantry during his distinguished career, by the end of WW1 having also being awarded the Albert Medal and

a DSO for his part in the First Ostend Raid in April 1918.

It was not until later in the war that the identity of the submarine was established. She proved to be SM *UC-66*, a German Type UC-II class mine-layer launched in July 1916 and commissioned into the *Kaiserliche Marine* (Imperial Navy) in November of that year. She only ever had one captain, *Oberleutnant zur* See Herbert Pustkuchen, a submarine ace who already had an impressive record as commander of previous submarines. During her short career between 11 February 1917, when her first war patrol commenced, through to 27 May when she was sunk, SM *UC-66* is credited with the sinking with both mines and torpedoes of up to 33 ships and badly damaging six others, representing the loss of 71,916 tons of shipping.

What remains of the *UC-66* today?

The wreck of *UC-66* was found in 2009, by mixed-gas divers, diving at a depth of 300 feet (90 metres). A damaged inflatable dinghy lay nearby on the seabed along with a pair of German Navy-issue leather overalls. The co-pilot's war medals are in the St Mary's Museum, along with an account of the incident. The only element of the RNAS station on Tresco remaining is the concrete launch slipway and the clubhouse restaurant known as the Flying Boat Club, which has many excellent photographs of the RNAS station before the base was de-commissioned in 1923. In the open fields south of Smith's Square on the seaward side, the concrete bases of the original huts used as living quarters can still be seen.

THE 'GRAND OLD LADY'
HMS *Warspite*

24 APRIL 1947 – MOUNT'S BAY

Ships have always been referred to with some affection as 'she', and it is no wonder that the battleship *Warspite* was known to everyone who served in her as 'The Grand Old Lady'. She began life in Devonport Dockyard when her keel was laid on 21 October 1912, one of five super Dreadnought *Queen Elizabeth*-class battleships, her sisters being *Queen Elizabeth*, *Valiant*, *Malaya* and *Barham*. She was ready for launch in 13 months, and by 8 March 1915 was commissioned and in service. She had a strange motto, '*Belli dura despicio*', which translates as 'I despise the hard knocks of war', which was perhaps appropriate since she earned the most battle honours ever awarded to an individual ship in the Royal Navy during her 30-year career in both world wars.

HMS *Warspite* was a result of the Dreadnought Race between Great Britain and Imperial Germany in the years leading up to WW1, each country determined to have the largest battle fleet. She was enormous, 32,590-tons, 644 feet (nearly 200 metres) long, her 24 oil-fuelled Yarrow boilers feeding turbines connected to four propellers, giving her a maximum speed of 24 knots, the equivalent of a fast cruiser. Each of the *Queen Elizabeth*-class were armed with no fewer than 24 guns, consisting of eight breech-loading 15-inch (38-cm) Mk 1 guns in four twin gun turrets, 14 6-inch (15-cm) Mk XII guns, 12 of which were mounted in casemates along the broadside of the vessel amidships while the remaining pair were mounted on the forecastle deck and protected by gun shields, and two quick-firing 3-inch (7.5-cm), 20-cwt Mk 1 anti-aircraft weapons. They were also fitted with four submerged 21-inch torpedo tubes, two on each broadside. The waterline belt to protect the ships from torpedoes was Krupp cemented armour 13 inches (33 cms) thick, the four main turrets and the main conning towers similarly protected, and each ship had multiple armoured decks ranging from 1 to 3 inches (2.5 to 7.5 cms) in thickness. *Warspite*'s crew numbered between 1,025 officers and ratings to man her for war in 1915, including pilots for her four small amphibious seaplane aircraft, and 1,220 while serving as a flagship after the war.

As part of the Grand Fleet, on 31 May 2016 *Warspite* took part in the Battle of Jutland, the biggest but most inconclusive sea battle between Britain and Germany in WW1. She was hit and holed 150 times during this battle and damage to her port-wing engine room caused steering problems with which she was plagued for the rest of her career. *Warspite* was in service in November 1918 to escort the surrendered German High Seas Fleet into internment in Scapa Flow following the Armistice and in 1919 she was allocated to the 2nd Battle Squadron as part of the new Atlantic Fleet, mostly based in the Mediterranean.

During the inter-war years, *Warspite* was refitted twice, emerging from the second refit at Portsmouth Dockyard in March 1937 as a virtually new warship, with her internal machinery replaced, a changed profile and new capabilities. Her 24 Yarrow boilers were replaced by six new Admiralty boiler rooms and geared Parsons turbines were fitted in four new engine-rooms, increasing her fuel efficiency by reducing fuel consumption from 41 to 27 tons per hour while maintaining a speed of 24 knots. The elevation of her main armament was increased by 10 degrees (from 20° to 30°), adding 9,000 yards of range, so that she could now hit targets at 32,300 yards (16 miles). Finally, her superstructure was radically altered, allowing two cranes and an aircraft hangar to be fitted; her tripod mast was removed and a distinctive armoured citadel built up to enclose the bridge.

When war was declared in September 1939, *Warspite* was recalled to the Home Fleet following the loss of HMS *Royal Oak*. From then on, until she last fired her main guns on 1 November 1944 after the invasion of Europe, *Warspite* was in almost constant action in all theatres of WW2. This included participation in both the First and Second Battles of Narvik off Denmark & Norway in 1940, returning to the Mediterranean to take part in the Battle of Calabria against the Italian Navy and then at the Battle of Cape Matapan in April 1941. Later that year she left the Mediterranean for the west coast of the USA where she was repaired again and re-fitted, before joining the Eastern Fleet at Trincomalee in 1942, remaining in the Indian Ocean to fight the Japanese surface fleets and to cover the landings of the Allied invasion of Madagascar that September. After returning to the UK in May 1943 she joined Force H with which she returned to the Mediterranean, covering the invasion of Sicily. She bombarded Catania to cover the 8th Army, then returned to Malta at high speed. It was there that Admiral Cunningham coined the nickname which she carried from that day on, signalling

'Operation well carried out. There is no question when the old lady lifts her skirts she can run.'

The repairs necessary to keep *Warspite* in service after determined efforts by German Dornier Do-217 bombers to sink her were massive and she was forced to return to Rosyth in March 1944. Her participation in the Normandy landings on 6 June was essential, and she returned to war with only six of her 15-inch (38-cm) guns serviceable, eight 4-inch (10-cm) anti-aircraft guns and 40 8-barrelled pom-poms. Her main armament opened a bombardment of the enemy coast starting at 5 a.m. on 6 June in support of the main landings. She continued firing until she had exhausted her stock of 300 shells, returning to Portsmouth for two days of intense re-armament and was back off the Normandy beachhead on 9 June. Further damage forced her return to Rosyth but *Warspite* was back in action off Ushant in August 1944, bombarding the German coastal batteries during the Battle of Brest. She fired her big guns at Le Havre, then moved towards Antwerp, shelling German strongholds on Walcheren Island in the Scheldt Estuary, before returning to anchor off Deal on 2 November, never to fire her guns again.

The damage HMS *Warspite* had sustained in her career from running aground, hitting a rock, shellfire, bombing, collision, ramming, fires, mines and guided missiles, all proved too much to retain her in service as the war in the Far East required more modern ships. Once the war was over, there was a proposal to retain her afloat as a museum ship, but eventually the Admiralty approved that she be scrapped. She was technically sold to Metal Industries Ltd on 12 July 1946 for scrapping at Faslane (the same yard that later broke up HMS *Vanguard*), on the Clyde, but before making her final journey she was required to go to Portsmouth Dockyard for the removal of her guns and other fittings.

Warspite was never to make it to Scotland. On 19 April 1947, she left Portsmouth under tow of two tugs, the *Bustler* and *Melinda III*, with only a skeleton crew of seven men under Captain Baxter on board. All went well until

Warspite: A forward gun turret before the barrels were removed prior to her wrecking.

midnight on 21 April when they met a south-west gale. The *Bustler*'s towing cable parted off the Wolf Rock lighthouse, and by morning the wind and tide had combined to push the battleship into Mount's Bay. By midday on 23 April the tug *Melinda III* was forced to slip her tow and the towing crew dropped one of the *Warspite*'s two huge anchors. It failed to hold, dragging across the seabed until the ship went ashore on Mount Mopus Ledge, an isolated reef a mile south-west of Cudden Point. The Coastguard called out both the Penlee and Lizard lifeboats, the coxswain of the former going alongside to advise Captain Baxter that it was now low tide and that at high water the tide would take her off the reef and put her ashore on the coast. As the tide rose so the *Warspite* did indeed float clear and went ashore on the rocks off Prussia Cove.

Coxswain Madron of the Penlee lifeboat *W. & S.* returned to the scene from Newlyn where the boat had sheltered overnight, and found conditions around the wreck appalling. She lay just a little to the east of the old smuggler's cove, starboard side to the shore with her bow pointing in to the storm and huge waves breaking over her side bulges and around 'B' turret. The only shelter which could enable any attempt to rescue the towing crew was alongside the ship's starboard quarterdeck, where there was a 40-foot (12-metre) wide channel between the wreck and the rocks. Coxswain Madron took his boat into this gap, pumping out oil to help subdue the waves as he went, until he was able to pass two lines to the ship. There now began the perilous job of keeping the lifeboat in one place long enough to take off the seven crew, which required the engineer to manoeuvre

the lifeboat's engine ahead and astern as they were thrown up in the air by 40-foot waves, sometimes looking down on the battleship's quarter deck, then down in a trough looking up at the ship's sheer side. The men jumped aboard the lifeboat as opportunity presented and six were saved, but then the seventh got cold feet and refused to jump. Finally he plucked up courage and leapt across the gap to safety. It had taken thirty-five hair-raising minutes to get them all off, the lifeboat returning to Newlyn Harbour at 7.45 that evening. For a remarkable rescue Coxswain Edwin F. Madron was awarded the RNLI's Silver Medal, mechanic John H. Drew the Bronze Medal, whilst the other six crew received the official certificate of 'Thanks of the Institution Inscribed on Vellum'.

This rescue was the first service of Edwin Madron as coxswain, and he was later presented with the RNLI's Maud Smith award for the bravest lifeboat rescue of the year: praise and recognition indeed, and well deserved.

It was now obvious that the *Warspite* was never going to reach Scotland, so that contract was cancelled and she was sold to R. H. Bennett, of Bristol, who did a deal with the Wolverhampton Metal Company of Wednesfield that they would break up the wreck where she lay. *Warspite* lay there rusting away for three years until 1950 when an attempt was made to refloat her. Twenty-four huge compressors pumped air into her sealed hull but she refused to lift off and over the reef. A second attempt in August was successful and she was towed around St Michael's Mount and beached in the shallows. An application was made by the salvors to Penzance Town Council in October to be allowed to place the wreck adjacent to Albert Pier for ease of access, but this was refused on the grounds of possible silting of the wreck, pollution, and the possibility of the wreck being abandoned. It was agreed the wreck could sit up to 2,500 feet (over 750 metres) away from the harbour entrance and lighthouse pier, but another attempt to move her made that November ended up with the wreck only 130 feet (40 metres) closer to shore near St Michael's Mount, and the tug *Tradesman* with 60 feet (18 metres) of wire cable around her propeller.

Salvage work then commenced using two permanent cranes on deck hired from MacSalvors, which made its name and reputation from the *Warspite* wreck. Cutting up a battleship is no easy task, especially with the thickness of armour plate she carried, and thermic lances and cutters had to slowly eat their way into her, great chunks of scrap metal being dropped into barges and landing craft alongside, which were towed away.to Penzance quay. Any WW1 battleship was going to have a fortune in non-ferrous brass, copper and bronze on board, apart from her four non-ferrous 10-ton propellers, and this was the 'icing on the cake' of the salvage operation. Her remains eventually disappeared beneath the surface and the salvage cranes disappeared by the summer of 1955. According to the contractors, she remains the largest salvage operation ever carried out in British waters. So ended the long career of the 'Grand Old Lady', an ignominious end for a type of warship which the world will never see again, the capital ships of the future being aircraft carriers and nuclear submarines.

What remains of the *Warspite* today?

Nothing remains of HMS *Warspite*, only a memorial stone which was placed near the sea wall at Marazion over 40 years after her sinking. The stone was unveiled by Admiral Madden along with a former crew member who recited a prayer. The inscription reads:

HMS Warspite 1915–1945.
Ran aground and broken up on these rocks 1947, her final haven known to all who served aboard her. As the Grand Old Lady, may she with many gallant shipmates rest in peace.
Erected by HMS Warspite Association.
Unveiled by Admiral Sir Charles Madden, DFC, CB.
September 25, 1992

Admiral Cunningham had one of her bells, the remains of her masts lie in a yard at Porthenalls House, Prussia Cove, and one of her 15-inch (38-cm) bronze gun tompions is on display in the Royal Naval Museum, Portsmouth. One of her aluminium gangways, complete with handrails, gives access to the dry moat around Star Castle, St Mary's, Isles of Scilly. Her brass nameplate is in The Wink pub, in Lamorna, Cornwall; a brass gangway nameplate sits in the entrance to a former captain's home in South Africa; her chapel door is displayed at the National Museum of the Royal Navy's Jutland exhibition at Portsmouth Historic Dockyard. The door was in fact rescued from the Seamen's Hostel in Falmouth and has been owned by the Royal Naval Association since 2012.

THE CAPTAIN WHO STAYED WITH HIS SHIP
SS *Flying Enterprise*

10 JANUARY 1952 – SOUTH-EAST OF THE LIZARD

There is a certain romance and heroism attached to a shipwreck when her captain, regardless of the danger he is in, decides to remain with his ship until she sinks beneath him. There have been many such incidents in the long history of the sea, including the SS *Titanic*, but a more recent West Country example deserves pride of place in this book.

The ship in question was the SS *Flying Enterprise*, a 6,711-tons survivor of World War 2, having been built in 1944 as the Liberty ship Cape *Kumukaki* by the Consolidated Steel Corporation of Wilmington, California. Sold to Isbrandtsen Company in 1947, she left Hamburg on 21 December 1951 for New York, carrying a general cargo and passengers. She ran into a storm on Christmas night when about 380 miles west of Land's End, and it was later found that a huge wave had caused severe structural damage. A crack had developed across her upper deck and down one side, causing her to list initially to 30°; by 28 December the cargo shifted, one of her holds flooded and she assumed

a dramatic 45° list to port. In response to her radio S.O.S signal MV *Sherborne* went to her assistance, but Captain Carlsen was reluctant to evacuate his passengers and crew to a British ship, preferring to wait until an American vessel arrived. The destroyer USS *General A. W. Greely* appeared that afternoon and between the two ships their lifeboats rescued the 40-man crew and nine of her ten passengers including two children, but one passenger, a Polish man called Nicolai Bunjakowski, had fallen overboard and drowned. The *Flying Enterprise*'s Danish-born but now naturalized American captain, Henrik Kurt Carlsen, was left alone on board and he refused to abandon his ship.

By 2 January 1952 a second destroyer, USS *John W. Weeks*, appeared on the scene and relieved the *Sherborne*, which continued her voyage to Manchester. Both destroyers continued to stand by the ship, for reasons which became apparent later. On New Year's Day a Royal Navy aircraft from RNAS Culdrose, Cornwall, had taken a photograph of the stricken ship, Carlsen alone on the afterdeck, clinging

SS *FLYING ENTERPRISE*

to a railing, waving and smiling as if he were a cruise liner passenger. The ship's port deck was now under water and the ship was listing at 60°. By radio Carlsen advised the world that he was tired but happily 'dining' on currant buns, beer and Rhine wine, and whilst he made nothing of it, he maintained the ship's log every day, recording events, the weather and even what rations he had consumed!

On 3 January the arrival from Falmouth of the ocean-going tug *Turmoil*, which had assisted a crippled cargo ship into Falmouth before putting to sea again to assist the *Flying Enterprise*, brought fresh hope that the ship could still be towed safely into port. Several attempts by the tug's crew, under the direction of her Master Captain Dan Parker, were made to pass a heaving line with an attached towing hawser to Carlsen, but each attempt failed. Then there was a split-second moment when the deck of the *Turmoil* and the port rail of the heavily-listing *Flying Enterprise* almost touched and the tug's acting first mate, 27-year-old Kenneth Dancy, despite not wearing a life-jacket, seized the opportunity to swing himself across, taking the end of the heaving line with him. Now it was Carlsen and Dancy together, and between them the two men managed to attach the towing hawser to the *Flying Enterprise*'s stern bollards and the *Turmoil* set off to tow her to Falmouth, some 300 miles (560 kms) away.

For six days and nights, though still listing at between 60° and 80°, the *Flying Enterprise* had found a new centre of gravity and the tow proceeded smoothly. On 6 January the *John W. Weeks* was relieved by another US ship, the *Willard Keith*, which supplied daily food rations to Carlsen

and Dancy via an attached line. A growing flotilla of other vessels nearby now included the French tug *Abeille 25* and at a further distance, as it was later disclosed, Russian ships. By 9 January they were only 41 miles (76 kms) from Falmouth and there were high expectations of reaching port where an excited crowd, which was following the story each day through newsreel footage, was waiting to welcome them. Three more vessels had joined the small convoy: the Trinity House *Satellite* vessel and two more tugs, *Dexterous* and *Englishman*, as well as a following flotilla of small craft packed with photographers and journalists.

But the weather conditions were worsening again. At 1.30 a.m. on the morning of 10 January, the tow line snapped in heavy seas. This time all attempts to reattach it failed and as the *Flying Enterprise* slowly turned over on her port side, Carlsen and Dancy finally accepted that they could not save her. Now wearing life-jackets, they made their way along her horizontal funnel and jumped into the sea, where they were soon picked up safely by the *Turmoil*. Less than 40 minutes later, the stern of the *Flying Enterprise* went underwater and her bow rose skywards. At 16.10, watched sadly by Carlsen from the cabin of the *Turmoil*, the *Flying Enterprise* sank to a cacophony of siren and foghorn salutes from the other vessels.

Carlsen, Dancy, Captain Parker and Commander O'Brien of the *Willard Keith* received a rapturous welcome when they were escorted into Falmouth the next day. On his return to New York on 17 January, Captain Carlsen was driven in an open car through the city to a 'ticker-tape' reception. Later he was awarded a Lloyd's Silver Medal for Meritorious Service in recognition of staying with his ship, which had prevented any third party from claiming the vessel as salvage. Kenneth Dancy also received great acclaim, 20,000 people turning out to give him a hero's welcome in his home town of Tunbridge Wells, and he too was awarded a medal from the American Institute of Marine Underwriters. In fact, he was not a regular crew member on board the *Turmoil*, having been on leave from his own ship at the time. He had never served on a tug before and only volunteered at the last moment to replace the *Turmoil*'s first mate who had been taken ill.

Carlsen was offered $250,000 for an exclusive story by the *Daily Express* newspaper, and received an offer of $500,000 to take part in a Hollywood film production, but he declined both, saying

> *'I don't want a seaman's honest attempt to save his ship to be used for any commercial purpose.'*

He returned to sea where he spent the rest of his career, as captain of *Flying Enterprise II* for many years. When he died in 1989, he was buried at sea over the wreck of the *Flying Enterprise* at his request. Captain Parker, the unflappable Master of the Southampton-based *Turmoil* who told the eagerly awaiting press that the episode had been 'just an ordinary job', was awarded an MBE in the Queen's Honours List the following June. Sadly, he only lived for another three years, dying in 1955 after an accidental fall off a bridge ladder on his tug. Kenneth Dancy married

Petronella van den Tempel, a Dutch woman, in 1956, gave up the sea two years later and settled in the Netherlands working for Phillips Radio and IBM. He died on 3 August 2013.

So why had Captain Carlsen risked his life by remaining on board? Ownership of the wreck is not in question while a member of the crew remains on board. Had the *Flying Enterprise* been completely abandoned, then the first individual to get aboard or the first vessel to take her in tow could claim salvage rights, and if the ship and her cargo could be saved, the financial rewards could be huge. The *Flying Enterprise* carried a cargo of 486 tons of coffee; 447 tons of rags; 39 tons of peat moss; 12 Volkswagen cars; antiques and antique musical instruments; typewriters; 447 tons of naphthalene; $600,000 in US bank notes and a further $200,000 in cash.

Supposedly, there were also 1,290 tons of pig-iron on board but it has since been suggested that this cargo was in fact zirconium, intended for use in America's first nuclear submarine, the USS *Nautilus* (SSN-571). This has never been officially confirmed but it is known that the US was actively acquiring zirconium and it is believed that the supplier was Philips in Eindhoven, the company that had the first patent on a process to obtain this high purity material and that the buyer was one of the companies intending to bid for the contract with the US Atomic Energy Commission. The loss of the *Flying Enterprise* was said to have set back the launch of the *Nautilus* by a whole year. Captain Carlsen affirmed that he took the cargo on board at Hamburg in sealed containers and was unaware of their real contents until he was informed some time after the event by Russian sources, which had been shadowing the *Flying Enterprise* before she sank. He always maintained that his sole reason for staying with the ship was that it is a captain's duty to do so until all hope is lost.

In 1960 the Italian salvage company Sorima obtained a permit to recover cargo from the wreck, now lying on her port side in a depth of 276 feet (84 metres). Sorima recovered some $210,000 of the estimated $800,000 of cargo, but a confidentiality clause in the salvage contract prohibited any release of the details, or any mention of zirconium. The company did reveal that they had recovered $61,000 in bank notes, but that a package of $100,000 could not be found.

What remains of the *Flying Enterprise* today?
The location of the wreck is 31 nautical miles (57 kms) south-east of the Lizard, and 41 nautical miles (76 kms) from Falmouth. On 22 June 2001 a Danish diving company called No Limit Diving visited the wreck and the Danish film-maker Lasse Spang Olsen made a documentary, 'The

Mystery of the *Flying Enterprise*'. Leigh Bishop, a one-time British fireman and acknowledged as an expert deep-wreck diver, researched the sinking position and was able to lead the expedition to the exact site. His photographs positively identified the wreck. Later, Leigh Bishop and US divers John Chatterton and Richie Kohler filmed the wreck for an episode of the BBC's History Channel TV series *Sea Detectives*, the deepest wreck dived in the 56 episodes filmed. Artefacts recovered went on display for several years in the National Maritime Museum, Falmouth, and an August 2018 edition of the BBC's *Antiques Roadshow* programme showed a life ring from the ship and a life-jacket, which may have been Carlsen's or Dancy's: poignant and valuable relics of this remarkable incident. There is a public house in Cork named the 'Flying Enterprise' after the ship.

Several books have been written concerning the incident, including *Rescue Tug: the Story of the 'Flying Enterprise' and the Salvage Tug 'Turmoil'*, by Ewart Brookes (Dutton, 1957); *Simple Courage – A True Story of Peril on the Sea*, by Frank Delaney (Random House, 2006); and *Carlsen of the 'Flying Enterprise'*, by Gordon Holman (Hodder & Stoughton, 1952).

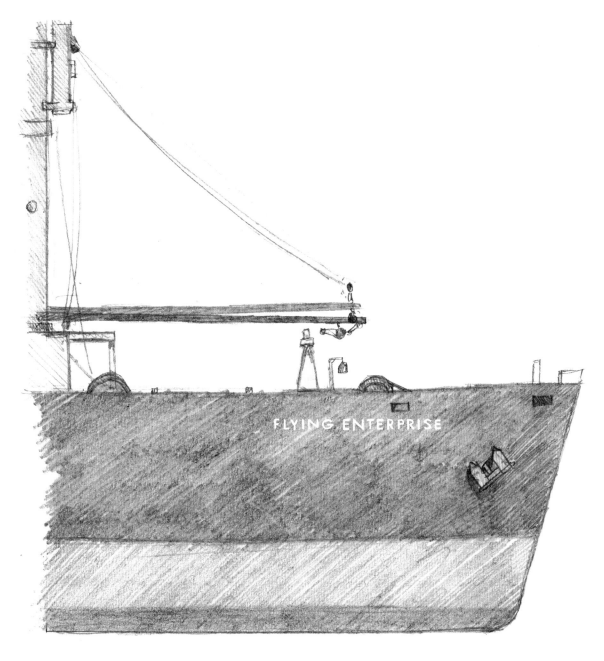

The *Flying Enterprise*'s bow

SS *FLYING ENTERPRISE*

THE BLACK TIDE
MV *Torrey Canyon*

18 MARCH 1967 – POLLARD ROCK, THE SEVEN STONES REEF

The *Torrey Canyon* disaster was not only the world's first major oil tanker spill; she was also the largest ship afloat at the time and hence the largest shipwreck, not only on the coast of Cornwall, but in the world.

This 974-foot (297-metre) long tanker left Kuwait on 19 February 1967 for Milford Haven in Wales, carrying 120,000 tonnes of crude oil. Due to her size she could not use the Suez Canal, so her passage took her around Africa, and on 14 March she passed between Tenerife and Gran Canaria. Here Captain Pastrengo Rugiati radioed the ship's agent who was acting for the owners, the Barracuda Tanker Corporation, a subsidiary of the Union Oil Company of California, requesting orders.

He was advised that it was imperative that the tanker arrive at Milford Haven by 23.00 (high water) on 18 March, otherwise it would be another week before the tide was high enough to berth and discharge. The unspoken message was 'time is money'. The earliest the ship could arrive using her planned course would be 17.00 on that date; however, their destination was still four days away and their rate of progress dependent on the weather.

The course set from the Canaries should have taken the *Torrey Canyon* five miles west of the Isles of Scilly, from where it was north-east to Pembrokeshire and the oil terminal at Milford Haven. In the evening of 17 March, the captain went to bed leaving the ship on auto-pilot and instructions that he be woken at 06.00 the next morning. Two things happened during the night: the notorious Rennell Current set the ship well to the north-east, and for some inexplicable reason the first officer changed her course from 018° to 012°. On waking, the captain expected to see the Scillies off to starboard: instead, the islands were visible to port and far too close. He ordered a return to 018°, now intending to take the alternative short cut between the Scillies and Land's End, very much aware of his deadline for arrival at Milford Haven. The course was then changed to 013°, but at 08.48 the watch officer clearly saw the rocks of the Seven

Stones Reef breaking ahead. He informed the captain who ordered the ship's helm to be turned hard to port, but with the autopilot still switched on the ship refused to turn. By the time anyone realised that the steering should be switched to manual to allow the wheel to be used, it was too late, and the *Torrey Canyon* hit the Pollard Rock at 17 knots, tearing open at least 14 of her 18 oil tanks. The order for her engine to be put full-astern achieved no change in her position; she was well and truly impaled from below, and was going nowhere.

A Mayday distress call brought out the Dutch salvage tug *Utrecht*, the rescue tug based in Mount's Bay at the time, but 20-foot (7-metre) seas made it impossible to get alongside to pass towing cables, so it was agreed to try again at high water. In anticipation of her being re-floated, her Polish engine room crew were ordered to start pumping out her oil cargo, and soon there was a slick astern six to eight miles long as 20,000 tons of crude was discharged into the sea. The government ordered the destroyer HMS *Daring* from Portland to act as guard-ship on site, to keep all other shipping away from the area, including Russian 'spy' trawlers. The Daring was then joined by two other warships which later commenced to spray detergent on the oil slick.

In London the Admiralty advised the government to set fire to the oil, but this drastic action presented problems. The Bermuda-based Barracuda Tanker Corporation wanted the ship refloated, whilst British Petroleum which had chartered the vessel and owned the cargo didn't want to lose any more valuable oil. With the vessel technically in international waters and outside British jurisdiction, the government's hands were temporarily tied. Even Maurice Foley, the Under-Secretary for Defence (Navy), said that there was 'no question' of deliberately destroying the super-tanker. By next morning the slick was 20 miles long; the ship was listing 8° to starboard and her crew had been taken off, so now she was derelict. At noon on 19 March a second attempt to pull her off failed but resulted in an explosion of fumes in the engine room which blew two members of the five-man Dutch salvage crew on board clean out of the ship and into the sea, killing one and injuring three others.

Even if she could be refloated there was no port prepared to accept the Liberian-registered *Torrey Canyon*. Within a week of the wreck, oil was coming ashore on Cornwall's beaches. On 26 March the ship broke into three pieces and her remaining cargo poured into the sea unchecked; only now would the salvage company accept that she was a total loss and that a decision as to future action was imperative. The only solution was to do what the Royal Navy had suggested earlier – set fire to the ship. On Tuesday 28 March, Operation Oil Buster was put into operation. Blackburn Buccaneer aircraft from RNAS Lossiemouth flew almost the length of the country to drop 42 1,000-lb (450-kg) bombs on the ship, but unfortunately a quarter missed the massive stationary target altogether. These were followed by Hawker Hunter jets from RAF Chivenor which dropped cans of aviation fuel onto the wreck to make the oil blaze, but high seas kept putting out the fire. Further bombing runs by Sea Vixen jets from RNAS Yeovilton and Buccaneers from RNAS Brawdy, as well as more RAF Hunters, this time controversially dropping napalm, continued to ignite the oil until the *Torrey Canyon* sank the next day.

The effect and extent of the oil pollution was horrendous, with 270 square miles of sea covered by the oil slick, whilst 120 miles (nearly 200 kms) of Cornish coastline was contaminated. The heavy crude oil rolled in like a black tide covering the rocks and beaches of Land's End and west Cornwall. Troops and volunteers worked on the beaches and coves until they were exhausted, scraping and shovelling the thick treacle-like oil, attempting to clean up the beaches before the Easter holidaymakers arrived. It was estimated that 15,000 sea birds died after contamination made them unable to fly; the white and black carcasses of seagulls, guillemots, cormorants and shags were everywhere, submerged in the evil, toxic, viscous gunge.

British Petroleum, which owned the *Torrey Canyon*'s cargo, also manufactured detergent, seen at the time as a first-generation oil dispersant. This was supplied to the government in industrial quantities, delivered initially in 40-gallon (180-litre) steel oil drums, which were rolled down quays and jetties onto warships, fishing boats and any small vessel prepared to assist. Supplied with hand pumps, these craft then went to sea and sprayed the oil, causing it to thin, then sink. There is a little-known story about these oil drums, thousands of which were left empty after use, creating a storage problem. A temporary solution was found by stacking them in huge 80-foot (24-metre) pyramids

on the airfield at RNAS Culdrose. Not knowing what to do with them, the government offered the empty drums for sale at 5 shillings each, and the owner and founder of Trago Mills, Mike Robertson, who had opened his first store in a shed in Liskeard, bought the lot, sat back and waited. As demand for detergent (eventually reaching 10,000 tons) was stepped up, it was delivered by road in huge tankers, then needing to be decanted into 40-gallon drums – which were suddenly in short supply! Now desperate, the government had no choice but to buy them back for £1 each, and Trago Mills' shrewd boss made a healthy profit without touching them!

Cornwall did not realise initially that it had got off lightly. Only 15% of the oil actually came ashore here; the remainder, due to currents and a freak absence of prevailing south-westerly winds, was deposited on the coasts of Brittany and Guernsey. Nineteen days after the wreck, the oil was so thick on Guernsey that it could be pumped direct from the sea into sewage tankers. It was then deposited in a derelict quarry, where much of it remains.

The wreck of the *Torrey Canyon* had some positive outcomes as it led to huge changes in ship construction, legislation and maritime law, as well as the creation of international maritime regulations on pollution, which were all long overdue. We now know that the use of detergent to disperse oil is the worst possible action as it creates a different, less visible kind of toxicity. Tankers are now built with double hulls, governments have developed reliable floating oil-booms to contain spills, and coastal councils have oil-spill contingency plans that were not even thought of in 1967. International law now imposes strict liability on ship owners without the need to prove negligence. Despite legislation, between 1967 and 2002 when the last major tanker spill occurred, there have been 24 ships which have each leaked more than 50,000 tons of oil into the ocean. The worst was the tanker *Castillo de Bellver* in Saldanha Bay, South Africa, in August 1983, when 252,000 tons of oil spilled into the sea. The *Torrey Canyon* remains the worst oil spill in UK history.

A Liberian inquiry blamed the wreck on Captain Rugiati, determining that his navigational misjudgement in taking the 'short cut' to Milford Haven was 'the proximate cause of the accident'. Rugiati presumably lost his Master's ticket, never to command a ship again. The British and French governments each sued the owners for £3 million, but Britain was only able to issue a writ by arresting the *Torrey Canyon*'s sister ship, the *Lake Palourde*, four months later in Singapore.

What remains of the *Torrey Canyon* today?

The remains of the wreck are scattered close to the Pollard Rock on the Seven Stones Reef, seven miles from St Mary's, Isles of Scilly. Part of her bow section was said to have been recovered and towed to Milford Haven where, after repairs, it became a floating bunker. Bronze blades from her propeller were illegally recovered, and one individual was taken to court and successfully prosecuted. Having been bombed repeatedly and then subjected to 51 years of storm and gales, little is recognisable. An unmanned Trinity House lightship still stands guard over the reef.

The *Torrey Canyon*.

MV *TORREY CANYON*

THE PENLEE DISASTER
RNLB *Solomon Browne* & MV *Union Star*

19 DECEMBER 1981 – BLACK CLIFFS, NEAR LAMORNA

Over the centuries Cornwall has witnessed more than 5,500 shipwrecks, equating to 20 ships lost for every mile of coastline. Each shipwreck is a tragedy in itself, especially if it involves loss of life, but nothing resonates with a coastal community more deeply than the loss of its lifeboat or crew. Cornwall has lost many brave individuals who were lifeboat men, and the Penlee disaster of 1981 carried echoes of what had happened at St Ives in 1938 and 1939, when two lifeboats and a combined total of 12 lives were lost from the same station within twelve months. The effect on St Ives was such that the lifeboat station closed down for a whole year.

Since 1913, the base for RNLI's operations in Mount's Bay was just south of Newlyn on the outskirts of the village of Mousehole, at Penlee Point which gave its name to the lifeboat station. Lifeboats could be launched into open water at all states of the tide down a slipway from the slightly elevated boathouse. The last lifeboat to operate from this site was RNLB *Solomon Browne*, a wooden, twin-engined,

47-foot (14-metre) Watson-class boat that arrived at the station in 1960. The Penlee disaster less than a week before Christmas 1981, which cost the lives of all eight members of the crew of the *Solomon Browne* as well as the five-man crew and all three female passengers from the 1,400-ton coaster MV *Union Star* which the lifeboat was trying to save, was mourned throughout the country as a national tragedy.

It began after dark on 19 December 1981 when Land's End Coastguard received a call at 6.04 p.m. on VHF radio Channel 16 from the *Union Star*, stating:

'I am approximately eight miles east of Wolf Rock. My engines have stopped, unable to start at the moment. Could you please have a helicopter standing by for us?'

The station repeated the location for confirmation, requested more details and was informed that there were eight people on board and that she was a 1,400-ton coaster carrying fertiliser. The ship then advised their intention which was to get the main engine started, but if this was not possible 'we will have to take everybody off and get someone to tow us in.' The *Union Star*, with her cargo of 1,250 tonnes of calcium ammonium nitrate in bulk, had set off two days earlier from the Dutch port of IJmuiden on passage to Arklow in County Wicklow on the east coast of Ireland. Although this was her maiden voyage, for her captain Henry 'Mick' Morton the passage down the North Sea, through the Dover Straits, along the coast to Land's End, then right hand down for the Irish Sea, was routine and normally expected to take a maximum of four days. But on this occasion Captain Morton had made an unauthorised diversion to pick up his wife Dawn and two teenage step-daughters, Sharon and Deanne Brown. Dawn was a seasoned captain's wife, used to ships and the sea, who sometimes accompanied her husband having signed on as cook. The two girls, aged 14 and 15, were on holiday from South Africa where they lived with their father, and had come to England for Christmas to see their mother and step-father.

Mick and Dawn had their home near Harwich, and at 8.30 a.m. on 18 December the *Union Star* was off Brightlingsea, close to Colchester, picking up Mick's family from a waiting launch, before turning south for the Dover Straits. The offer of a passage on the coaster over Christmas had greatly appealed to the girls as a novelty, giving them family time together on board and later in Ireland. However, Mick had not obtained official permission for them to be on board, as that would have involved insurance complications with the owners – but what could possibly go wrong?

The 32-year old skipper was a seaman through and through, having held his Master's ticket since the age of 27. He was highly regarded by the company, Union Transport PLC of Kent, and to be given command of a brand-new ship was official recognition of his ability. To have his family aboard for this short trip was the icing on the cake, but he was worried about the weather. There was a severe weather warning for the Plymouth sea area, possibly a southerly gale 'increasing force 8 to storm force 10'. He had two choices: to continue and hope that they could round Land's End and put the wind astern, or to divert to Falmouth and anchor; but he had already lost seven or eight hours in collecting his family and could not afford to lose any more time. True, they were not due in Arklow till Sunday when the port would not be working anyway, so perhaps he could get away with it? He decided to continue on passage.

As the sea got up, for the women this pleasure cruise now became an ordeal of endurance as the *Union Star* rolled and heaved, but the five-man crew were used to such conditions. The ship was now close to the Wolf Rock lighthouse, the worst of the passage hopefully behind them, and in an hour they could turn north and run before the wind, but it was not to be. As with all motor vessels, diesel engines are prone to problems with water in their fuel tanks as well as air locks. Ventilation is achieved by pipes sticking up well above deck level fitted with a goose-neck valve to allow air in but not sea water swilling about the deck. The engine's fuel system itself has filters and pumps, sight glasses and bleeding valves, so what exactly failed was not known for some hours to come. At around 5.45 p.m. the engine faltered, coughed, started again and then stopped; only later was the fault found to be caused by water in the fuel. When the engine stopped, so did the electrical generator; hence all the lights went out, her 24-volt emergency battery system feeding only the gyrocompass, radio telephone and a minimum of emergency lighting. George Sedgwick, the engineer, assisted by the captain, attempted to re-start the engine but soon exhausted the compressed air cylinders used to turn the engine over, leaving the ship helpless in an increasingly rough sea. Just one of her two auxiliary generators run for ten minutes would have easily re-filled the air cylinders, but neither could be coaxed into life.

Following the captain's radio message to the Coastguard at Land's End, the rescue services co-ordinated by the recently opened Falmouth Coastguard Centre were asked to 'stand-by' but only in an 'Alert' phase. A Sea King Rescue helicopter at RNAS Culdrose on the Lizard peninsula was alerted; as was the Dutch tug *Noord Holland*, which in those days was on permanent stand-by in Mount's Bay for such emergencies. She was requested to be in readiness to assist but the *Union Star* had not as yet initiated a 'May Day' distress situation. Captain Buurman of the rescue tug advised Falmouth Coastguard that he was prepared to offer the Union Star a Lloyd's Open Form, a 'tow and pay' agreement, the cost appropriate to the service rendered. It was open-ended in that it was 'no cure – no pay', a standard international agreement. The tug skipper spoke to the *Union Star* direct on Channel 9, but no immediate agreement was reached.

Falmouth Coastguards were now having trouble contacting the launch authority for the Penlee lifeboat. The RNLI Secretary was out for the evening, there was no reply on the telephone from his deputy, and the third authority's telephone refused to ring. With no alternative they got in direct contact with the lifeboat coxswain, Trevelyan Richards, advising him of the situation and requesting that the lifeboat anticipate a launch and that the crew 'muster in the boathouse'. The Coastguard ended the conversation with the impression the lifeboat would be prepared for immediate readiness, but things at Penlee were not that simple. The boathouse was old, small, cramped, cold and without any basic facilities, so it was customary for the crew once contacted by telephone to remain on stand-by either at home or await a second call if elsewhere.

The captains of the tug and the *Union Star* had a disagreement over the radio, the former not prepared to weigh anchor without first agreement over the Lloyd's Open Form, Captain Morton insisting he put to sea but only to stand by in case he was needed, at no cost. The standard Master's Manual stated specifically that 'in the last resort' a ship's master had the authority 'to act without higher instructions if necessary to engage salvage assistance', but Morton was worried about 'saving face' and the effect on his career. Captain Buurman had no such reservations and after consulting his head office he weighed anchor and headed for the *Union Star*'s position, reasoning that his tug was safer in deep water than in Mount's Bay anyway. At 6.27 p.m. Coastguard Sector Officer Don Buckfield was asked by Falmouth Coastguard to man the radar at Land's End to determine the *Union Star*'s proximity to land. Buckfield's fix on the coaster showed that the ship was now only 3½ miles (5.5 kms) from the rocks, drifting north at 1.5 knots.

Captain Morton then agreed over the radio with Falmouth to upgrade their situation to a 'Pan-pan' broadcast, meaning 'urgent help required but not in imminent danger'. The next level up is 'Mayday' – 'grave and imminent danger' – when all protocols are forgotten and all available services respond, whether requested or not. Falmouth Coastguard now called Plymouth's Search and Rescue Co-ordination Centre and requested that the helicopter scramble immediately. At the same time the *Union Star*'s head office authorised Captain Morton to accept the tug's offer of a Lloyd's Open Form without hesitation.

So a second hour ticked away, with the tug still some distance from the *Union Star*, and the Penlee lifeboat still in her boathouse with her crew ashore elsewhere. Then, at 7.37 p.m., things began to happen. Sea King helicopter R80, whose pilot USN Lieutenant Commander Smith was on exchange from the US Navy, was now airborne with four crew aboard. Its task, to take off the women and children from a coaster, appeared simple. There was no 'Mayday'; the vessel was not sinking; it seemed a routine call out – at first.

The night was moonless, dark and it was pouring with rain, the wind speed over Mount's Bay gusting to 80 knots and more. On reaching the search area and dropping down to 400 feet (200 metres), the helicopter crew were astonished to find sea-spray filling the air at that level. The waves were 40 feet (12 metres) high and the coaster, firing red flares, was now only two miles offshore.

At 7.50 p.m. Falmouth Coastguard rang the Penlee lifeboat's Coxswain, Trevelyan Richards, to request an immediate launch of the lifeboat, at the same time ordering the Mousehole Coastal Rescue Company to assemble and stand by. It was left to the coxswain's mother to call out the lifeboat crew. She found James Madron, the mechanic and Second Coxswain, at home; Nigel Brockman (the assistant mechanic) was watching a ladies' darts match in the British Legion along with Gary Wallis; John Blewett (the emergency mechanic) was at his daughter's 15th birthday party; Barrie Torrie and Kevin Smith were watching a film; and the landlord of the Ship Inn, Charlie Greenhaugh, was doing what landlords do on a busy Saturday night. Once the maroons went off, Mrs Richards knew that her job was done. Seven men turned up initially instead of eight, and Nigel Brockman's son Neil volunteered to fill the gap but the Coxswain rejected him, saying

'no more than one from each family on a night like this.'

Then Charlie Greenhaugh arrived, and the boat now had its full experienced crew. All eight men had bidden their families goodbye as usual, manned the boat and went out into the night.

Helicopter winchman Steven Marlow found himself swinging in huge arcs, with the gale screaming around him, over the stern of the coaster which was rising and falling

136

on 60-foot (12-metre) waves and rolling at 40°. The biggest hazard was the ship's mast which was 50 feet (15 metres) tall and in danger of spearing him or even the helicopter. Three times they made a pass at the ship's stern where a crewman was holding a female hard against a locker awaiting rescue; then a huge wave threw the ship into the air, the mast missing the helicopter's rotor blades by less than 10 feet (3 metres). At 8.08 p.m. all the ship's lights came on, the engineer having managed to restart a generator, and the visibility improved. Six times the helicopter attempted to pass a 'high-line' to the ship but endangered itself with each pass. Now less than a mile from the rocks, Captain Morton told R80 he was going to drop an anchor. At great risk, a crew member crawled across the foredeck to the forecastle, knocked out the pin and her starboard anchor ran out, but the cable parted like a piece of string as the anchor took hold. The port anchor was then dropped with four shackles of cable, which dragged across the seabed but slowed the ship's drift towards shore.

Both the tug and the lifeboat arrived on the scene at the same time, 8.43 p.m., but it took only one look for the tug master to realise it was hopeless. The sea conditions made it impossible for anyone on the coaster to take a towing cable on board and attach it to her forecastle bollards. To get close enough to pass a tow line the tug needed to be on the coaster's lee side, but Captain Buurman was not prepared to risk his vessel between the casualty and the rocky foreshore, now clearly visible. Also, now that she had an anchor deployed, the *Union Star* could only be pulled clear if someone could slip the cable, which was clearly impossible in these conditions. The tug stood off, her captain aware that his journey had been a waste of time. That left the Penlee lifeboat as the last hope. Lifeboats, like tugs, prefer to effect rescues in the lee of a casualty, where the ship offers some protection. They can then pass lines to the vessel and hopefully survivors can scramble or jump into the lifeboat. But Coxswain Richards had no choice but to put his lifeboat against the coaster's weather side where most of her crew were waiting with lifelines; then the next 60-foot wave reared up and they moved off.

The crew of the *Union Star* then streamed a drogue or canvas sea anchor, drifting down before the wind on her port side, in an attempt to slow down the vessel. The lifeboat was being thrown against the ship's side repeatedly, but the two decks were never level for long enough to save anyone. The wind was now gusting to 100 mph (160 kmph), with the coaster only 200 yards (180 metres) from the cliffs and the helicopter still overhead, its landing lights illuminating the scene. Captain Morton suggested that the crew and passengers take to their life raft, but Coxswain Richards told them to stay put, still hopeful of a rescue.

Then the *Union Star*'s anchor chain parted, and she swung round beam-on to mountainous seas. The lifeboat ran in twice more, and on the second attempt the sea threw her bodily up in the air so that she landed squarely on top of the coaster's hatches, her propeller spinning, for a brief second high and dry; then another wave appeared, the coaster rolled and the lifeboat slid off stern first, unharmed. The helicopter R80 made two final attempts at a rescue, but conditions were even worse. The mast of the coaster rose and fell, whipping back and forth, and missed the helicopter's rotors by a whisker. It was time to abandon any hope of an air-sea rescue, and R80 lifted clear and backed away.

On board the *Union Star*, Morton ordered everyone out of the wheelhouse onto the deck, where they clung to the ship's rail, each wearing a lifejacket. At that moment, displaying incredible seamanship, Coxswain Richards threw his lifeboat against the coaster's side and eager hands dragged as many survivors as they could over the rails to safety. The two vessels separated again, leaving behind at least one, possibly two, orange lifejackets in the sea, and two people still clinging to the coaster's rail. The *Union Star* was now only 50 yards (45 metres) from the rocks. The time was 9.21 p.m.
The lifeboat reported to Falmouth Coastguard:

'We got four off at the moment, male and female. There's two left on board –'

Then there was a dreadful crash and the message ended, unfinished. The helicopter crew saw her afloat and upright after that call and, relieved that some lives had been saved, turned back to base. The tug master saw the lifeboat high in the air silhouetted by the *Union Star*'s lights, then everything went black. Her lights disappeared as the sea threw the *Union Star*'s starboard side against a ledge which, acting as a pivot, lifted her up and over, capsizing like a child's toy.

At 9.22 p.m. Falmouth Coastguard called the *Solomon Browne* but received no reply. They continued to call her until 9.41 p.m., then asked the tug if they had heard anything. The reply was a negative. Don Buckfield and the Coastguard Cliff Rescue Team were now overlooking the upturned *Union Star*, so Buckfield donned a harness and was lowered over the cliff. The gale was blowing spume, diesel and fertiliser into his face; then he saw a red light in the sea. He was hauled back up the cliff, then lowered again in a different location, where he saw that the light was attached to an empty red RNLI lifejacket – which spoke volumes.

The Auxiliary Coastguard at Penzer Point, a little further along the coast towards Lamorna Cove, reported a light heading into Mount's Bay. With the timing right for the lifeboat returning, the Royal National Mission for Deep Sea Fishermen in Newlyn was opened and hot drinks prepared. An ambulance and the police were on hand, and everyone waited in anticipation, ready to welcome them back, but they never arrived. R80 helicopter returned and searched the coast for 90 minutes. They even radioed 'Penlee lifeboat, if you read me fire a flare', but the message went unanswered.

The RNLI headquarters at Poole then authorised a multiple lifeboat launch, from St Mary's in the Isles of Scilly, Sennen Cove and the Lizard, to search for the *Solomon Browne*, now posted as 'overdue'. Even before daybreak, coastguards were finding masses of wreckage in Lamorna Cove: air-boxes, blankets, clothing and – even more grim evidence – timbers painted in the distinctive RNLI colours. A flotilla of fishing boats and another helicopter joined in the search but found only wreckage. The Scilly lifeboat was called to St Michael's Mount, and towed back to Newlyn the entire stern of the missing lifeboat.

Coxswain Trevelyan Richards' body was found floating between Tater-Du and Lamorna, and helicopters picked up those of *Union Star* crew member Manuel Lopes and Sharon Brown. Charlie Greenhaugh was found in Lamorna and the coaster's engineer, George Sedgwick, off Penzance promenade. Dawn Morton's body was found days later also at Lamorna, as was RNLI assistant mechanic Nigel Brockman's. RNLI crewman John Blewett was not found till Boxing Day. Not all the bodies of the 16 victims were ever recovered.

Two funds were set up: the 'Penlee Relief Fund' in Penzance and the 'Fishermen's Fund' in Newlyn. Money from the latter was collected, counted, divided eight ways and immediately given to the appropriate relatives. The official 'Penlee Relief Fund', which after Christmas stood at nearly £2 million, was set up as a charity with trustees, and immediately ran into trouble. If the fund was administered under charity regulations, which would not allow the eight families 'to improve their standard of living', then they would get nothing; if a donation was deemed to be a gift, it was subject to tax! This was not what the donating public wanted. In the event, the government and the Charity Commissioners relented and agreed that the fund which eventually reached £3 million would be classified as private and shared between the families of the eight RNLI crew members. The families of the five crew of the *Union Star*

received £45,000 between them from their company appeal fund.

A Memorial Service was held on 22 January 1982 in Paul church, overlooking Mousehole, and was attended by the Duke (as President of the RNLI) and Duchess of Kent and many local dignitaries. Three weeks later a larger and more formal service was held in Truro Cathedral, attended by Prime Minister Margaret Thatcher and her husband.

The inquiry into the loss of both vessels took 29 days at a cost of £1.25 million. The findings, delivered on 27 May 1982, concluded that the loss of the *Union Star* was caused by a combination of engine failure, severe weather and capsize of the vessel. The inquiry paid tribute to the crew of the *Solomon Browne*, whose loss was found to be

'in consequence of the persistent and heroic endeavours by the coxswain and his crew to save the lives of all from the Union Star. Such heroism enhances the highest traditions of the Royal National Lifeboat Institution in whose service they gave their lives.'

Coxswain Trevelyan Richards was posthumously awarded the RNLI's gold medal, while the remainder of the crew were all posthumously awarded bronze medals. The lifeboat station itself was awarded a gold medal service plaque.

The replacement lifeboat for the *Solomon Browne*, costing £450,000, was paid for by retired businessman and owner of Radio Rentals David Robinson, who had already given away £26 million to good causes. All he asked in return was that the replacement lifeboat should carry his wife's name, *Mabel Alice*, which she did. As she was designed to remain permanently afloat, instead of being launched from a slipway like her predecessors, the Penlee lifeboat station was closed and a new station opened at Newlyn Harbour, where the *Mabel Alice* lay at moorings until her 'retirement' in 2003. For many years the Coxswain of the *Mabel Alice* and her successor the *Ivan Ellen* was Neil Brockman (son of the *Solomon Browne*'s assistant mechanic), whose life had been spared by Coxswain Trevelyan Richards' refusal to risk the lives of more than one family member on that fateful night.

What remains of the *Penlee* disaster today?

The wreck site lies beneath the coastal footpath which runs from Mousehole to Lamorna, between Tater-Du and Boscawen Point. Nothing remains visible of either vessel, the sea reportedly having torn the wrecks apart. The four-bladed bronze propeller of MV *Union Star* was removed by divers and now hangs in the clubhouse in Northampton.

The tragedy is commemorated in various places, including a side chapel of St Clement's Methodist church in Penzance and a memorial garden adjacent to the former Penlee lifeboat station. Every year on 19 December, the famous Mousehole Christmas lights are dimmed for an hour in memory of the 16 people who lost their lives that night. The names of the eight RNLI crew members of the *Solomon Browne* are inscribed on the RNLI Memorial at its headquarters in Poole.

The definitive account of this dreadful tragedy may be read in Michael Sagar-Fenton's book *Penlee: the Loss of a Lifeboat*, first published in 1991 by Bossiney.

Union Cove.

RNLB *SOLOMON BROWNE* & MV *UNION STAR*

THE TROUSERS THAT CAUSED A SHIPWRECK
RMS Mülheim

22 MARCH 2003 – LAND'S END

Sailors are notorious for superstitions, which include claims that sailing on a Friday, whistling on board, changing a ship's name and countless others will bring bad luck. Whilst ships are more likely to be lost for more practical reasons such as fire, explosion, collision, navigational error, drunken captains, storm or enemy action, who would believe that the loss of a modern ship fitted with every navigational aid could have been caused by the Chief Officer's trousers? Yet this was the freak official reason for the wreck of the German cargo ship *RMS Mülheim*. This must be unique in maritime history, although there are some similarities to the fate of MV *Cita*, a bulk carrier with 128 containers lost on the Isles of Scilly on 25 March 1997. On that occasion the wreck was attributed to the watch officer having fallen asleep with the ship's auto-pilot switched on but the radar alarm off, so that she drove ashore on St Mary's at 12 knots.

Launched as the *Zeus* and registered in Antigua as a flag of convenience, she was built in 1999 by the Tulcea Shipyard in Romania, but had her name changed to *Mülheim* by her German owners only two months later. A general bulk carrier of 1,599-gross tons, she traded for four years around Europe. On 22 March 2003 she was on a voyage from Cork, in the Republic of Ireland, to Lübeck, Germany, carrying 2,200 tonnes of scrap car plastic from the chopped-up remains of dashboards, door liners, roof linings and seats etc. She also carried old car batteries and new containers of paint.

It was early in the morning and still dark as the ship approached Land's End, the weather forecast being 'moderate visibility with fog patches'. Apart from engine room staff below, the only man awake on board was the Chief Officer on the bridge, seated in a comfortable watch chair. He went to stand up for some reason, perhaps to get a cup of coffee or merely to stretch his legs, when a cargo pocket on his trouser leg caught in a control lever on the chair, he lost his balance, fell over and hit his head, becoming unconscious. How long he was in this state is uncertain, but when he recovered consciousness and stood up he found the ship close inshore and heading for the steep cliffs at Land's End.

She drove ashore at approximately 5 a.m. in Gamper Bay, between Land's End and Sennen Cove. Although the Sennen Cove lifeboat was launched and was first on the scene, with the Land's End Coastguard Cliff Rescue Team on the high ground overlooking the wreck, the 'Mayday' radio call also brought a Search and Rescue helicopter from RNAS Culdrose, which airlifted the six-man Polish crew to safety. They were dropped off at Sennen Cove car park, and taken first to the Lifeboat Station and later to the Seaman's Mission at Newlyn, leaving the wreck abandoned.

Daylight revealed the *Mülheim* was leaking diesel into the sea, her double bottom having been torn open on the rocks, and it was later estimated she had already lost some 75 tonnes of fuel. However, the spillage of diesel was a minor pollution problem for the authorities compared to the potential threat of 2,200 tonnes of plastic chippings spilling into the ocean, which would cause catastrophic pollution. Hence the immediate priority was to save the ship if possible, and otherwise to recover the cargo before the sea could claim it. The wreck lay under 70-foot (22-metre) high cliffs on a very rocky coastline, exposed to and at the mercy of any westerly wind. After all, it was March – a month notorious for gales.

The well-known Dutch salvage company Wijsmuller was invited to consider taking on her recovery. Although she was still an intact ship despite underwater hull damage, the Dutch experts needed to work quickly to try to remove as much of the cargo as possible before the hull broke up against the rocks. Initially, on 10 April, they placed a small 'jack-up' rig with a crane alongside the wreck using a large grab which discharged the plastic into barges before being towed away. However, this presented serious problems. As soon as the wind got up, not only was it impossible to keep the barges alongside the rig but the wind was blowing plastic all over the place. By now some 400 to 500 tonnes of plastic had escaped the ship's hold and was floating on the surface of the sea in a great bank, much of it ending up on Land's End beaches. In fine weather Wijsmuller, using the grab and barge method, could probably have removed the entire cargo in a matter of two or three weeks, but in the prevailing conditions an alternative solution had to be found, since the jack-up rig method had to be abandoned after only six days.

With the serious potential threat of an ecological disaster, the government ordered the Maritime Salvage and Intervention group to work with its own Maritime and Coastguard Agency and Cornwall County Council to co-ordinate the recovery of the cargo. They settled for a conveyor belt between the cliff top and the wreck, and the problem of the plastic blowing about in the wind was solved by loading it into giant, sealed canvas bags. To allow the salvors access to the wreck a rope walk-way was set up from the clifftop and, as wind and tide allowed, men went into the ship's hold, loaded the bags, and sent them to the cliff top where waiting lorries took them away.

They managed to work for 25 days until 11 May when a severe storm commenced to cause the ship to break up and recovery ceased, with only an estimated ten tons of cargo remaining in the hold, most of the batteries and paint having been recovered in the early stages. On 23 May the *Mülheim* was declared a constructive total loss by the underwriters. By 30 May all work on the ship ceased, the conveyor belt and walk-way were dismantled, and the *Mülheim* was abandoned to the sea, just another shipwreck of which Land's End has seen so many over the centuries. No wonder the Romans called the area 'Bolerium', meaning the 'seat of storms'.

During the summer months any shipwreck on the coast is bound to attract inquisitive sightseers, and the *Mülheim* was no exception. The tourist attraction complex at Land's End welcomed the additional business as holidaymakers made the spectacle an excuse for a day out. Clifftop fields were turned into temporary car parks by enterprising farmers, which in turn attracted stalls selling pasties, sandwiches and soft drinks. The local shops and cafés later admitted that they had had a bumper season. The *Mülheim*'s bad luck after changing her name turned out to be good luck for Cornwall's tourist industry!

What remains of the *Mülheim* today?

On 7 October 2003 the wreck broke in half, and by the end of that month both halves were pushed by heavy swells, further demolishing her structure, into an inlet known as Castle Zawn. To the present day much remains identifiable, with most of her superstructure and wheelhouse intact as well as most of her stern, amidst a vast amount of rusting steel plates. It is still possible to climb down to the wreck, but dangerous and not recommended. An account of the shipwreck appears in the author's booklet *Cornwall's Shipwrecks: North Coast* (published by Tor Mark Press, 2010).

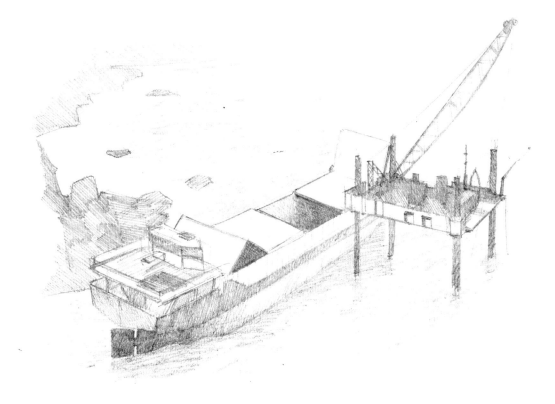

RMS Mülheim

RMS MÜLHEIM

ACKNOWLEDGEMENTS

The author acknowledges with thanks and appreciation the contribution made to this publication by the following individuals: Sir Tim Smit of the Eden Project and the Charlestown Shipwreck Centre for his Foreword; Peter McBride; David McBride; Kevin Camidge; Sean Kingsley; Innis McCartney; Peter Holt; Tony Randall; Ivan and Heather Corbett; Bridget Larn for proof reading and suggestions and Kevin and Kristen Davey for their support and friendship. Additional thanks to Ron Johns, publisher, for his commissioning of this project and for his patience, encouragement and advice during the production stage.

RICHARD LARN OBE

ST. MARY'S, ISLES OF SCILLY. 2019.

I would like to say a special thank you to Ron Johns of Mabecron Books for including me on this project, plus the rest of the team: Debbie Watson, Richard Larn, Kate Dinn and Keryn Bibby. Thanks also to Hugh Hastings. I would also like to thank my Mum and Dad for their continuous encouragement, and my partner Ula for her unwavering support, and putting up with the constant smell of oil paints and thinners.

OLIVER HURST

BATH. 2019.

Men of the St Agnes Lifeboat Crew

N

W   E

S

• *Bandoeng*
Eemland
Gaasterland
Jacatra
Noorderdijk
Zaandijk
Normanna

All sunk approximately
37 km NW of this point
(page 102)

The

ISLES

of

SCILLY

T.W. Lawson (page 88)

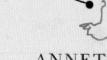

ANNET

BISHOP ROCK

Association (page 32)

Schiller (page 70)